Homecoming

Crossing the Bridge to the Soul

Volume 1

Homecoming

Crossing the Bridge to the Soul

Volume 1

Keith Anthony Blanchard
(Sri YahNahVah)

6TH
BOOKS

Winchester, UK
Washington, USA

JOHN HUNT PUBLISHING

First published by Sixth Books, 2020
Sixth Books is an imprint of John Hunt Publishing Ltd., No. 3 East St., Alresford,
Hampshire SO24 9EE, UK
office@jhpbooks.com
www.johnhuntpublishing.com
www.6th-books.com

For distributor details and how to order please visit the 'Ordering' section on our website.

ISBN: 978 1 78904 411 9
978 1 78904 412 6 (ebook)
Library of Congress Control Number: 2019941184

A CIP catalogue record for this book is available from the British Library.

Design: Stuart Davies

UK: Printed and bound by CPI Group (UK) Ltd, Croydon, CR0 4YY
US: Printed and bound by Thomson-Shore, 7300 West Joy Road, Dexter, MI 48130

We operate a distinctive and ethical publishing philosophy in
all areas of our business, from our global network of authors to
production and worldwide distribution.

Contents

Preface I	1
Preface II	5
Introduction	9
Initiation	13
Following My Divine Script	15
Make No Mistake ...	25
Walk Into the One	29
Integration	65
Dreams, Dreams, Dreams	67
India Bound	89
Lessons In Love	106
That Feeling!	109
Deep Into the Rabbit Hole	126
Swinging Back and Forth	134
Amen To That!	141
What A Great Day To Be Alive!	146
Stoking the Fire Within	153
Thank You, Grace!	156
Apply, Integrate, Transcend, Be	160
Sai Ram, That Lady Is Me!	163
The Return of Christ	169
Oh, My God!	177
Going Home	185
All Is Well	189
The Layover	192
Home Sweet Home	198
Do You Believe?	201
Clarity	204
Come – See – Reflect	222
About the Author	223

I lay this book at Your Lotus Feet, O' Lord,
as an offering that it may touch those
who read it in the same way You have touched me.

~ Om Sri Sai Ram Guru Deva Datta ~

The Divine Principle: Anchoring Heaven On Earth
Editor/Copyshaper/Withwriter: Stella Steele
Additional editing: Brian Steel, Stacy McKinley
Cover design by: Keith Blanchard and Rikk Flohr
Formatting: Mike Matheson
Contact: info@fleetingglimpse.com
Cover assistance: Fleeting Glimpse Images

For the Love of God: A Spiritual Journey
Editing: Linda Chaplin Westbrook
Additional editing: Cindy Somerville and Stella Steele
Cover concept: Keith Blanchard
Formatting: Cecil McDaniel

To contact The Center of Light:
Send e-mail to: keithanthonyblanchard@gmail.com
Web Site: www.keithanthonyblanchard.com
YouTube: www.youtube.com/centeroflightradio

Preface I

It's August 19, 2003, as I sit at my computer to write about how *The Divine Principle: Anchoring Heaven On Earth* came to be.

As I reflect back on my life from my present vantage point, I can see that a deliberate hand has affected it always, but because I was unaware of its influence, I lived in an ongoing state of turmoil and fear. At various times in my childhood I did actually manage to slow down enough to sense these promptings, especially when I served as an altar boy every Sunday in church. Then, when I was a teenager, I even attended seminary school and thought seriously of becoming a Catholic priest. But that isn't what I really wanted it seems, because I soon reverted to my unconscious ways.

As the years passed with their many ups and downs, I came to regard the few good things that happened to me as my life's highlights, and I despised the bad ones because I thought they only proved that things always got worse. And I was perpetually worried about how, or if, this kid was ever going to find his way.

In my late twenties I finally had to admit that I was living with way too much chaos inside and all around me. Since nothing else I'd done had ever worked to help me get things in order, I decided to at least try to surrender the rest of my life to God's Will. After I'd made my decision to get more faith in my life, I went about living it, even though I didn't know for sure if anything was ever going to change for the better.

It was around then that God got my attention big time, but He didn't come to me as you might imagine. There was no burning bush. I didn't have a talk with George Burns. And Jesus didn't appear above my bed. No, God came to me through someone that I'd been involved with for ten years.

Towards the end of our relationship, things were not at all good between this woman I claimed to love and myself. In fact, they were terrible! All we did was fight. Our relationship had become one of no communication, patience or tolerance.

It was just awful because, through all our troubles, I still loved her. And through it all, I prayed to God that we could find some peace.

I should have been clear about what I asked for because, to my amazement, one day my longtime love dropped the big bomb, telling me that she wanted to end our relationship. That began a landmark period for me, even though, through my pain, I couldn't see it at the time. Now I know that that's when I truly recognized God as a presence in my life for the first time.

Early on in this time of transition, I began to meditate every day in an effort to find some sense of stillness. To help myself stay in that peaceful space and to make myself available for any God-manifestation that might come along, I soon intensified my practice. Whatever I was doing must have worked because one day God actually spoke to me – and I could actually hear His Voice!

"Good morning, Keith!" was what I heard when I was abruptly awakened on that cloudy June morning in 1996. In my dazed state, I thought that my wife at the time or a friend was nudging me to get up so they could tease me for being so lazy. But when I sat up in bed, I could see no one there. Then the Voice spoke again, "I am inside of you. Yes, it is true that I am here with you and you are here with Me!"

At that moment, I fell back on the bed, my eyes closed, and I found myself standing in the Presence and Light of the Divine. As I tried to collect myself, my first thought was, "What do I do with this?" The Voice responded, "I shall tell you. Sit on the sofa, press RECORD on your tape player, close your eyes and let your mouth move." I did what the Voice instructed, and to my astonishment, out came volumes of the most far-out material I'd ever heard. When I opened my eyes after that first God-session, all I could think was, "Oh shit!"

Later that afternoon when I shared what had happened with my then brother-in-law Kevin, he suggested, "Keith, maybe you should go meet with Robin." Robin was an acquaintance of his with the gift of sight – a psychic. Kevin assured me that Robin was genuine and very good at what he did and that he could most likely tell me much more about the phenomena that had begun to appear in my life. Though I'd never met this person before, I determined to let what he said help me decide what to do next.

I made an appointment to see Robin as soon as I could.

When I got to his home the next afternoon, he answered the door, greeted me warmly and invited me upstairs to the little sanctuary he'd created where our reading would take place. As we got settled, Robin asked me to tell him my zodiac sign and then asked to look at my left palm. To this day I remember the first thing he said, "You are being told to write a book, aren't you?"

"What! Oh my God, then it's real!" I was so blown away that I had a difficult time concentrating on the rest of the reading. In fact, I don't remember any of it except what he said about writing that book.

I left Robin's house still not certain about what I was going to do other than begin to write down all the words that the Voice was speaking into my mind. Over the next few years, questioning the whole time why I was doing this, something kept happening that helped me to accept my fate. "What was that?" you ask. "What helped you finally and wholly surrender to your path?"

Well, after hearing the Voice for a while, I began to have strong premonitions – visions – that would fade in and out as I diligently transcribed on the computer all that was coming to me. It was as if God was handing me a complete plan that told me what I needed to do in order to help myself and others.

To this day, those visions have continued to reinforce my trust throughout this entire process. And the more I've let myself trust, the easier it's been for me to hear and feel the Love that could only be emanating from that wondrous Being.

Now I humbly and gratefully share with you, my readers, all the incredible things He told me – the splendor, joy and wisdom of all I've received. And I wish for you, too, a life full of the love, peace, prosperity and bliss I've come to accept.

Preface II

As a young boy, no doubt, I had an insatiable appetite – an unquenchable curiosity about the Creator, the universe and my sole/Soul purpose for being on the Earth. And, it's been a lifelong pursuit to curb my hunger for answers to four simple, basic questions that were gnawing at me.

Throughout all of my soul searching, I'm confident that I've come to the point that the answers I've found are solid, balanced and are in alignment with the Highest Good of each and everyone's Divine Script. Here are those questions and my answers.

"Where did I come from?"

You came from the Great Ocean of Divine energy ... the universe ... the stars. We are all Seeds of our Loving Creator planted on the Earth. Our celestial nature and free will allows us to germinate, grow, sprout and bloom, until the season when we are able to unfold the Love of God.

"Why am I here?"

I was told over and over in my daily meditations that the only reason we are "here" is to live the best life possible. But, for that to happen, we must live our passion. There's no other reason for our birth.

If God is Love, then it should make sense to you that, when you do what you love, the River of Life moves through you and puts you on course to the bridge between Heaven and Earth. I feel blessed to have come to this realization early on in my adult life.

"Who am I?"

This question, which is probably the biggest one in the batch, took me a while to "get" and accept. Let's examine it more closely.

If we came from God and will one day consciously return,

who are we now? If God is the beginning and the end and we are in the middle of all that, who are we? If God is omnipresent (present in all places at all times), who are we? Point to yourself. Point to God. Can see the connection? At our essence, that is (the truth of) Who we are.

I'm aware that this kind of talk may cause some people to run away as fast as they can in fear. That's because they don't understand the Laws of Spirit nor the Laws of Physics. I'm also aware that it can sometimes be tough to see your own Greatness. But believe me, you are more than you even realize. Your passionate, sincere search for your own answers is what'll bring you to this realization for yourself. What helped me to reach my epiphany was understanding the simple idea that God is the Energy which connects all things together and, if we were separate from that, we couldn't exist.

"Where am I going?"

Wherever you want! The choices are infinite. But, if you ever want to get where you are truly wanting to go, you must first know where you come from, why are you here and who you are. Only then will you be prepared to get to where you are going.

I often wondered when I would sit down to write another book. The fact is, after writing my bestseller, *The Divine Principle: Anchoring Heaven On Earth*, I knew I needed some time off to absorb, digest, relax and rejuvenate before I went through the process of doing it all over again. Well, the appropriate time must be now as I sit here typing away.

The story I'm about to tell you is true. And, I invite you to be open to it and allow yourself to feel what I felt on my quest to find God (my Self) in India.

As a professional musician, in 1999, I earned the best income for myself to that point. As I recall, I had a lot of money stapled in stacks of hundreds under my mattress, only because the bank I was using seemed to not know the difference between what mine was and what was theirs. Even so, the financial abundance in my life at that time paled in comparison to the spiritual abundance of what was coming down the pike.

Just when I thought that my life couldn't get any better, the phone rings out of the blue.

"Hello?" I answered.

"Hi, Keith. You don't know me, but I felt compelled to call you. I heard through a mutual friend that you want to go to India to see a holy man that came in a dream, inviting you to come see Him. Can I offer you a free, first-class round-trip ticket to India so that you can do just that?" she said.

That phone call changed my life forever!

That is the type of miracle that most people think only happens to a chosen few. Well, I'm here to tell you that there are no chosen few and that I'm just like you. This beautiful manifestation came to me because of the passion and sincerity I put into everything I do. Do you have the fire to make that kind of miracle happen in your life?

One day, as the time of my leaving for India was near, someone handed me a book telling me that it would make for a good read, as well as prepare me for the trip in many different ways: like what and what not to expect and what to do to not get sick. I didn't really have any expectations surrounding the trip, except to come back fully charged. And so, I decided to call a few clinics about getting shots that would protect me from anything I may be susceptible to from being in a foreign land. The prices for such shots were reasonable, but my hesitation was not because of the shots themselves. I came to realize that, if God invited me to come India and sent me a ticket to prove it, then surely, that same Grace would protect me and keep me safe. Needless to say, I didn't go to the clinic.

The journey you are about to embark on will take you to India where you will be in the presence of an Avatar (Divine Descent) by the name of Bhagwan Sri Sathya Sai Baba. You'll come to know of the magic, mystery and power of this Holy Man, and through me, experience what it was like to be there firsthand.

The chapters of me in India are written from a present tense perspective so that the impact of what you read will be greater, keeping true to the emotions that I was feeling at any given time. In this way, it will allow for a more exciting read, as well as open you up to the Miracle of Sai Baba through my eyes and heart.

Introduction

Crossing the Bridge To the Soul

We have all heard the saying, "Time flies when you are having fun." Well, My Friend, I can attest to that. Where *has* it all gone? From my experience, it hasn't passed me by as we normally perceive time to do. It just seems to have vanished! Today, as I am writing this, I am grateful to find myself deeper into an Infinite Space where time is a simple play of Divine Consciousness.

From the "time" I started writing my bestseller *The Divine Principle* in 1996 and completing it in 2009, I have learned so much from the wisdom that moved through my vessel. For the years that followed, I continued to live in the brilliant Light of those teachings, which I have no doubt readied me for the next plateau. I consider that phase of my life as, "The Initiation Into Spirit."

From the years 2000 to 2014, I was working on a book about my pilgrimage to India to see a Divine incarnation by the name of Sathya Sai Baba. *For the Love of God: A Spiritual Journey* was the beginning of the Rising Phoenix within me. Going back to 1996 and coming forward into 2014, I have experienced so much expansion that I almost could not contain myself. I consider that phase of my life as, "The Integration of Spirit."

About three and a half years ago, I was watching over a friend's house while they were in England. One day, I was sitting on the sofa in silence, thinking of what I could do to alleviate my boredom. When all of sudden, a Voice spoke to me from within saying, "Keith, grab your phone, go sit by the fireplace, turn on the video recorder and 'go at it.'" I immediately I got up, went over there, sat down on a pillow and "got right to it," not knowing what was about to unfold.

The first thing that welled up in my heart was to talk about how, "You Can Have It All." After looking into my cell phone, and taking some deep, intentful breaths to connect, I could feel the Voice begin to fill me inside as it did when I was writing *The Divine Principle*. For the next two years, that Presence began to consume me ... literally!

Since then, I have been doing a live video series on social media called *Center of Light Bursts*. These presentations are off-the-cuff, allowing the Voice of my heart to speak. One by one, as people gather in the virtual room, they experience this Divine Love pour through my being into theirs. It is such an amazing and beautiful thing to witness, watching them at every gathering burn with a Divine Fire for Radical Transformation.

After reviewing the playback of my first eight videos, I came to realize that something I was unaware of had begun to occur. I was the one becoming more and more radically transformed! A new book was already being placed within me, so I contacted my marketing director, Renee Brown. I hired her to transcribe all that came through these sessions, and we began editing the message into book format.

Lo' and Behold! I'm now working on my next literary love titled *Radical Transformation*. This powerful soon-to-be released wisdom has led me by hand and heart to the Golden Door entering the Kingdom of the Soul. Being in this heart-space daily is what has caused time not to flee from me, but utterly disappear.

As I reflect upon the last two years, I realize that, this time, the Voice has not only come to speak to and through me, but has come to be with me as Me. Yes, the Dove of Peace has descended into my heart at last, and along with that perching has come the grace of an ever-expanding awareness. This phase of my life I consider, "The Graduation With Spirit."

Through this declaration, my dedication and vow to you is this: I Am my, "You Can Have It All!" I now wear the Golden Ring on my finger, symbolic of my marriage with the Divine. I cultivate this relationship at every possible moment through my commitment to live a life of service to all.

But here's the thing! My olive branch gesture is that you reach for and join me in this sacred union yourself. And when you sincerely intend to do just that, the Dove of Peace and Everlasting Light will wipe the cobwebs of time from your mind and the darkness of fear from your vision. You, too, will find yourself crossing the bridge to the Soul and reside in the Garden ... at last.

The powerful journey you are about to embark upon will take you between *The Divine Principle* and *For the Love of God* and back again. Why? To create a timeline of the unfoldment process that I underwent to where I am today.

It is my intention and vision that this two-volume lamplight will spark *your* Initiation, Integration and Graduation. It is my blessing that you will know from bones to Soul ...

THIS IS YOUR HOMECOMING!

I Love You,
Keith Anthony Blanchard (Sri YahNahVah)

Seek Ye
The Kingdom Of God Within

Man is born with a great thirst and a deep hunger for Ananda
(Bliss). He knows that he can get it, but he knows not from
where. He has faint memories of his being the heir to the
Kingdom of Ananda. But he does not know how to establish his
claim to his Divine Heritage. Something in him revolts when
he is condemned to die, to suffer and to hate. It whispers to
him that he is the child of immortality, of Bliss and of Love. But
man ignores these promptings and, as one exchanges diamonds
for dirt, he runs in search of meaner pleasures and sordid
comforts.

You should be in perpetual contact with God.
Let the pipe that leads into the tap, which is you,
be connected with the reservoir of His Grace,
then your life will be full of unruffled content.
Without that awareness of the Constant Presence,
any service that you do to others
will be dry, barren.
Be aware of It, then any act of service
will yield plentiful fruit.
Every person is a spark of the effulgence of God.
God is dancing in every cell of every being.
Do not doubt this.
Do not ignore this or dispute this!
This is the Truth!
The entire Truth.
The only Truth.
The Universe is God.
All this is He, His body.

– Baba

Initiation

Following My Divine Script

What is the first memory you recall? My earliest one is of an event that took place before I was on the planet. I can actually remember waiting in line to be born, surrounded by an infinite number of souls waiting to do the same. No matter where I would look, all I could see was beautiful, light energy readying to leap into the swirling vortex that takes us from "there" to "here."

Another thing I remember about the experience is that all the excitement and anticipation floating about from the entire dynamic is what fed the whole of the system – somehow sustaining it.

In contrast to all that was taking place toward the front, there was another phenomenon happening behind me. There were waves of colorful, soul energy coming back from their brief trip to Earth (those who had died) only to get back into the line for another leap into the vortex, while some would ascend to another level entirely.

The earliest memory I have of being on the planet is getting bathed in the kitchen sink. I think we all know someone who can remember that. Sometimes these memories and feelings of mine are so strong that they literally launch me to a particular past moment. This point is integral in understanding the real message of this book.

As a little boy I was happy. The parents and siblings I'd selected this time around on Earth were great. My mother and father loved their six children and raised us to the best of their ability to be self-reliant and responsible. Now mind you, some of that parental love over the years took the form of a pop on the butt when needed, but, all in all, we were the quintessential family.

At the age of six, I started to become increasingly aware of myself and my surroundings. But something would begin to happen to me anytime I would hear music. When any musical vibrations would hit my ears, my body would begin to move and I'd start to bang on the table pretending to play drums, all the while singing at the top of my lungs.

To get me to dance for the relatives, Mom would open the hi-fi stereo (You know, the one she forbade me to touch!) and play the song *Wooly Bully*, by Sam the Sham and the Pharaohs. She knew that whenever I'd hear that song, I'd hunch down and go into this body shaking, arms swinging side-to-side kind of motion, giving everyone who watched a big laugh. Oh, yes! It was fun for a while.

After about a year, when the "Look at our little musical child!" wore off, the volume of the music and my banging was frowned upon. My guess is they didn't want to continue to add to the noise that already existed from living in a house with such a large family.

Mom was great at budgeting the money and keeping the Blanchard machine greased so that it would run as smoothly as possible, while Dad was the provider and did it in a wonderful, loving way.

One of the few luxuries we had other than ham once a month was my parents would take us kids to the VFW Bowling Alley on Barrow Street. I so loved going there because of the expanse, all the neon lights and the volume of the jukebox.

One day, I asked my brother, Kerry (who is the oldest), about a song that he played on his stereo from time to time. "What song are you talking about, Keith? Can you sing me a little bit of it?" he asked. I tried with all my might to think of the lyrics and the melody, but not a word would come out.

Later that evening, Mom and Dad loaded up the family into the Buick Skylark and we headed for the bowling alley. But, on this particular night, something was going to be different – the Love of God through the revelation of my Divine Script.

I clearly remember I was standing at the foul-line with both hands on a six-pound bowling ball, about to throw it down the lane from between my legs – and that's when it happened! It was a sound I'd heard only once before and was music to my ears. Out of that jukebox came ripping and roaring the song I'd asked my brother about earlier in the day. What song was it? It was The Monkees' *Last Train To Clarksville*. And boy, let me tell you ... that tune, that jukebox and that volume did a number on that little guy! I saw the truth of who I am and knew then and there, even at six years old, my life was complete. But, to get a standing ovation this time around, I'd have to follow my Divine Script and act It out. I had to become a star.

A few years later, around the age of eight or nine, I recall how I began to think about things a little more deeply – "Where did the vision of my life's path come from? Why is that thought in my head in the first place and what does it want from me?" I know now that these simple questions were instrumental to get my mind to open so I could eventually move into my heart and live my purpose.

From my current vantage point, I can see without a doubt that a life of music and spirituality were cast for me, and because I'm playing my part, the True Being of who I am is emerging.

At ages nine and ten, my desire for something beyond this world seemed to be present. So, I decided to don the clothes of an altar boy, hoping I would be fed answers to the new, deeper questions that began to spring up in my consciousness.

I really enjoyed being an altar boy and the few perks it offered, such as sneaking sips of wine, eating a few unblessed communion wafers when no one was looking, and of course, checking the weekly bulletin to see if my name was in it to serve again the next week. There was something about my name being "in lights" that made me feel good about myself and the idea that I'd done at least one thing of everlasting merit. And so, for the next few years, I went to Holy Rosary Catholic Church to do all the things that "good" Catholics do as their way of worshipping God.

My final year of serving as an altar boy was my most fulfilling time up to that point. Though I did learn a lot about the great spiritual teacher, Jesus, and the life thereof, it was not where I'd learn true compassion and my role to be of the Highest Service.

My greatest spiritual teacher was my sister, Cheryl, who was two years older than me. When she was ten, doctors diagnosed her with scoliosis, only to find out later that she had a condition known as Friedreich's ataxia (a disease of the nervous system).

Cheryl was everything to me. I loved her genuinely, simply because she was my sister. I found great joy in helping her with whatever she needed ever since her life (and ours) started to change. As she got a little older, she began to wobble whenever she walked and I helped her. Then she got a little bit older and needed a walker to move around and I helped her. Then she got a little older and needed a wheelchair and I helped her. Then she got a little older and wasn't able to take care of herself and I helped her by being a tough, little guy kicking anyone's ass who'd criticize her!

Cheryl passed many years ago, and even though she is no longer here on Earth, I don't in any way feel disconnected from her. The love and light her beautiful soul have shone on me is at the seat of my very core. Cheryl and I are unified through compassion.

I was twelve years old when my dad put a guitar in my hands for the first time. Although I did play drums in the school band from fifth grade all the way through high school, strumming my dad's Gibson Dove guitar is what got me jazzed. It had so much sound and melody that I couldn't wait to pull it out of its case and play along with him. I played that guitar in the morning, at night, and especially, when I would talk on the phone with girls to try to impress them.

A few years later when puberty began to bang hard on my

hormonal door, it brought with it the desire to chase girls even more. Now an adolescent with a new driver at the wheel, I soon realized that my guitar playing would likely help me to land a girlfriend. Heck, I was a little cocky, hot guitar player who had a few talent show winnings under his belt and was ready to take on the world.

At the age of fifteen, I started my first rock band, Sassy, consisting of all my buddies. We were a combination of two bands swapping members in and out depending on who was available for the gig that was booked. All in all, whatever the configuration, we sounded pretty good. We often played at "Skateland" in Houma, LA, school dances and at the airbase (a park) every Sunday, always packing out this little gazebo that sat in a big open field.

Enter my first girlfriend, Darla, who came along at sixteen. She had brown hair, big brown eyes and was beautiful! We met that summer at South Terrebonne High after the first school band rehearsal for the upcoming new year. I was a drummer from Ellender Memorial School and she was a flag girl from Oaklawn Junior High. After a quick introduction from a friend, she and I traded phone numbers and began to spend time together.

Six months into our dating and just before Homecoming, I was standing at my locker when Darla dropped a huge bomb on me. "Keith, I want to break up with you." I immediately became nauseous and faint-like. When I collected myself from the initial blow, I went to the school office, called my mom and asked her to pick me up and take me home because I was a sobbing mess. After I got home, I went straight into my room and began to talk to God. "Please, no … I can't bear this … it hurts too much!" I lamented for hours, days, weeks, even months.

In hindsight, I'm able to see how Darla's breakup with me was one part of my Divine Script. Her purpose was to walk into my life and introduce me to the joy that comes from living in the heart and the pain that comes from living in the head.

Sometime later after I jumped the abandonment hurdle, when I felt ready and stable for the next chapter of my life, I got back on the horse called "Purpose," and rode that baby quite a distance. I decided to go to a seminary school and thought seriously about becoming a Catholic priest. That is, until Jennifer walked into my life.

Jennifer and I genuinely liked and loved each other. She was a good girlfriend and had a great family. They took to me rather quickly and cared for me. They sheltered me, fed me and loved me, providing me with what I needed to live comfortably in their home. But after I got settled in, the Director of my Divine Script would begin to redundantly sound off in my head.

The voice was telling me about the two choices before me. Not that any one of them would've been right or wrong; it's just that, one followed my script and the other didn't. I was trying to decide between Jennifer, music and a rock and roll lifestyle, or to pursue God with the whole of my being. I chose to be with Jennifer and the lifestyle. We were together for about five years when the fire within me for any spiritual truth had flickered out. All the while, things between Jennifer and I became increasingly unstable.

In 1988, at the age of 24, on a whim I decided to climb aboard a Ryder truck with some friends and head to Memphis, Tennessee to live out my dream of becoming a rock star. Don't get me wrong. I had great friends, loved my hometown, loved the food, greatly loved my family, and I played in a popular band called Sorce. But, because Jennifer and my relationship was not working out and I had a dream to realize, Memphis seemed to be the carrot the universe was dangling in front of my nose. It was the greatest decision I've ever made in my life!

Leaving everything and everyone that I'd known behind, bravely, I traveled to the Land of the Delta Blues to live and become a working musician. I won't kid you for a minute about how I was scared out of my pants! I had no money, no car, no job, no girlfriend to lean on like I did with Jennifer – I had nothing but my dream and that seemed to be enough.

About two weeks after arriving in Memphis, the phone rang. "Hey, Keith? It's for you!" someone in the house shouted. "I wonder who in the world that could be?"

"What the hell are you doing in Memphis, Keith?" Jennifer asked upset and pissed.

"Living here and I ain't coming back!"

"Get your butt home!" she demanded.

"If you want to be with me, you'll have to come where I am!" I exclaimed.

After talking on the phone to her for about an hour, she considered transferring to Memphis. Four months later, Jennifer moved here and we continued with our relationship.

In the early 90s, I had two musical opportunities. The first one was a move to Seattle to join a band named Fifth Angel who was signed to Epic Records. The other was a two-month all-expense paid music gig in Hawaii – one of the highlights of my life and another important part of my script.

The island of Oahu was such an enchanting place I felt alive and at home there. After learning my way around, I'd often go to the North Shore at dusk, meditate on the beach by the water's edge and listen to Enya's *Shepherd Moons* album through headphones. The more I did this, the more I found myself becoming conscious of the seed that was planted years before. And the whole time I was in Hawaii, I could feel that seed germinating – readying to break through the topsoil of my life. I knew that when I'd return home, my life would be different in many ways.

Four months after I got back from Hawaii, Jennifer called me over to sit next to her on the couch and said, "Keith, I don't want to be with you anymore." Back into the pain I went. "Please, no … I can't bear this … it hurts too much!" I started talking to God again, lamenting for hours, days and weeks, and this time, for two years. Although I didn't see it at the time, Jennifer's exit was another part of my Divine Script – a change in path that would eventually lead me to everything I've ever wanted.

I can't begin to tell you of the needless pain I inflicted upon myself by trying to reignite a candle that has burned out. Eventually, I realized that it was never going blaze again and my only choice was to let it all go and trust that one day, somehow, my Phoenix would rise from the ashes.

Into my life walks Mike M., a co-writer of my script. Though Mike and I knew each other before Jennifer and I broke up, it seems that his role was to help lay out a smoother transition for my next chapter.

One night, in 1991, after my band's rehearsal, all the guys were going over to Chris' (the drummer) house. I was never asked to join them before because they knew I wasn't really into the "New Age stuff" they were into. But that night, for some reason, I was invited to come along. I said sure, thinking that all we were going to do was just hang out and party. Boy, was I wrong!

No sooner had we sat down in Chris' little upstairs room, than my bandmates and Mike began to talk about that "weird stuff." I just sat there, drinking my drink, listening to them go at it. But eventually my curiosity was piqued, because the things Mike was saying seemed so relevant to what I was going through.

After a few minutes, I asked if he could interpret a dream I'd had in which Jesus appeared to me and told me the word "Yam" three times. Mike asked me if there'd been more to my experience and, if so, would I share it. I said, "Sure."

"It was really weird," I said.

"In what way?" he asked.

"Jesus seemed to be behind me and up towards the ceiling, but I could see Him perfectly. At the same time, I could feel myself floating up there, too. But I didn't want any part of that, so, I somehow made myself wake up."

"Is that it?" Mike asked.

"Yep, that's it," I told him.

"Guy, that is so very cool!" he said. Then he got up and walked straight to the bookshelf, selected one book and brought it back to where I was sitting. He opened it to show me the meaning of "Yam" – the sound of the spiritual heart (the heart chakra), and his gesture touched me to my core. Yes, I knew in my own heart of hearts that something had awakened and there was no turning back.

From that evening on, whenever I was feeling down from obsessing about Jennifer, I called Mike and found much comfort in his words. Not only did he help me see things in a more realistic light, he also seemed to have an uncanny way of getting me to open up so that, for the very first time, I could begin to see myself/Self.

One day he asked me, "Without judging yourself, Keith, tell me, do you like your life?"

I said, "Hell no!"

His next question was, "What are you willing to do to have peace?"

I told him, "At this point, I'm willing to try anything!"

"Then prepare yourself for miracles," he said.

For the next hour or so, he laid out some principles I could begin to work with. But at the same time, he suggested that I not believe anything he was saying. "Just let the manifestations speak for themselves." I had no idea what he meant.

Even so, that very day, that week, that month, that year, as I began to put these new ideas into practice, I could see the little miracles that Mike had told me would take place if I kept to my "I'm willing to do anything for peace!" intention. But even though everything I was learning felt right, every once in a while, some part of me put up resistance.

You may ask why. Four reasons: I knew that everything I thought I knew would have to change. I knew that I'd have to take full responsibility for the mess I'd made of my life. I knew that, because of my unresolved emotional issues, my life was sure to get worse before it got any better. And, here's the real kicker – I was frightened because I didn't want my new "I am God" attitude to piss God off! But I was determined to change, no matter what it took.

I began to meditate daily as Mike had said to do. I can honestly say that the more I practiced meditation, the more my life improved. That alone has helped me stop feeling like a victim and to live more in harmony with God.

Mike entering my life was definitely part of the Divine play. It had to be! And, it's my hope that by the time you flip through to the last page of this book, you'll see how your life, and all life, is An Act of God.

Make No Mistake ...

MAKE NO MISTAKE ABOUT WHO I AM.

I
Am
God

I have no particular name; they all belong to Me. I am all things –
All that is. I am the Universal Generator of Supreme Knowledge
and Divine Energy. I am You! I am everything you can perceive
and everything you cannot. I am the Choreographer of the
Human Dance. I am the Conductor of the Cosmic Symphony.
I am the Universal Playwright. I am the Almighty, the Most
High, the Creator. I am Love. I am all Teachers who have ever
come bringing information about love and peace. I am Jesus the
Christ. I am the Buddha. I am Krishna. I am Sathya Sai Baba.
I am the All-knowing, All-pervasive and All-seeing Eye. I am
Clarity. I am Union. I am the Eternal. I am the Absolute in and of
all things. I am the Atma, the Soul and the Tree of Life. I am the
Only One. I am Jehovah. I am that I am.

God
Am
I

I come to you imbued with Love and Light, Joy and Might! My
purpose is of the highest calling: to give you the precious gifts of
My Words and My Love so that you can share them with others
and inspire them to join you in carrying out My mission.

MAKE NO MISTAKE ABOUT WHO YOU ARE, MY BELOVED
KEITH

Hello, My Friend, how are you today?

"Fine." (*thinking to himself*)

I am waiting ...

"For what?" (*still thinking to himself*)

For you to begin.

"Begin what?"

Transcribing what you have to say, Keith. This book will be unbalanced if no one knows what you are thinking.

"You're right – I have so many questions!"

I know. That is why this is your forum as well, a place for you to speak your own mind and heart. And I shall answer all that you ask, provided it serves you.

"Why me? Why did You come to me?"

Why not you? Keith, you have worked long and hard to get to where you are now – open to all possibilities of Spirit. You are ready.

"For what?"

To help Me write a book about universal truth. Can you deny that you have elected to come to the earth plane to carry out this very purpose – to share My words with as many people as you can?

"I'm a little overwhelmed, but, no, I can't deny that I've sought this path."

I know that My recent arrival in your life has seemed both a blessing and a curse – a rose under your nose and a thorn in your side. When I first made audible contact, you were very excited, but you were also quite frightened because you did not know just how to handle what was happening to you. You had moments when you thought you were special, and moments when you feared that you were schizophrenic.

"Yeah, I've definitely been through a lot!"

Yes, all your life I have watched you bounce back and forth between these two extremes in hopes of finding your True Self. I come to you now because you have exhibited such passion to live a better life. I come to you because of your newly awakened love for Me – and because of My Love for you.

You see, you and I are not different at all, for we both share the same intention – to chip away at the beliefs that you thought were set in stone and to carve you into the most beautiful masterpiece ever known – God.

Keith, I cannot begin to tell you the ways your life will change, nor can I allay all your worries about what may happen when this book circulates. In fact, it is likely that you will be deluged with confusing feelings. But I can tell you that I am here to help with all that may be troubling you and that, for the rest of your life, I shall guide you so that you can play your part in making the world a better place.

Even though, right now, you have no idea what you will do with what you are beginning to receive, it is enough for you to know that the message comes from God. Fret not about those who may doubt you or scoff at what you say, for they may not be ready to hear it. You can put your mind and heart at ease nonetheless, knowing that everyone walks the path at their own pace.

As I pour My Light into your mind and My Love into your heart, just make a supreme effort to remain open, relaxed and aware in every moment, even when I am speaking directly to others. Only then can you integrate all My information.

"How am I doing so far? I mean, the path I'm on?"

You have already done some mighty fine work on yourself, Beloved, but now the *real* work begins!

Between now and forever, I ask that you gather people, one at a time if you have to, but gather them do. Embrace each of your brothers and sisters without discrimination and treat them with the same Love I bestow upon you, be they "enemies," friends, relatives or strangers. Embrace every little spark of God.

Your journey will be smoother if you accept the fact that, through everything, I am here.

"I'm so glad to be able to ask You all the questions I've wanted to ask if I ever got the chance. Y'know, the ones that could change the world if we had those answers."

Well, you are not the only one with questions. Here are some I ask *you* to ponder:

From whence did you come?

Did you have an identity before you were born?

Why were you born?

What is this energy that was given a name at birth?

Who are you now?

Where are you going?

MAKE NO MISTAKE ABOUT WHO YOU ARE, MY BELOVED ONES

It is no accident that you hold this book in your hands! Now that you have it, I encourage you to take full advantage of it, for within its pages you will find everything you need to understand your True Self and your relationship to the Spirit you call by many names. The words My scribe has written herein are to prepare you for the change that is already underway. Consider this work an instruction manual for your return to God.

Those of you who choose to live by the ideas and principles I present herein will awaken from your dream of separation and shift into a higher reality that will enable you to consciously reunite with Me. So I implore you to not only read these words with your eyes, but with your heart, for doing so will open you even more to receiving My Intent and My Energy – All that I am.

I have miracles for every one of you. Seek them with sincere intention and I shall grant you the awareness that will cause them to appear.

Fortunate are you to be the frontrunners and to read about the Divine changes soon to come. Blessed are you to receive the Divine Principles that will empower you. Privileged are you to learn about the return of Master Jesus and other Masters of My Most Holy Light.

Walk Into the One

Are you ready to begin your journey, Keith?
"*I am so ready! What are we gonna talk about first?*" (excitedly)
Webster's Dictionary.
"*Huh ... why?*"
Because it tells of your language, and its words will help Me to clearly and precisely convey my ideas. Using this resource will give you a deeper and broader perspective of any principle I am targeting.
"*Okay.*"
Here is our first definition:

Union
An alliance for mutual benefit.
The bringing together of two entities into a whole.

Scripture speaks of God as the Living Word, the Essence of life itself. "In the beginning was the Word. And the Word was with God, and the Word was God." (John 1:1) How hard can it be to see how people create grief, fear and division within themselves by denying this most profound truth?

I come to you now to teach you how to accept Me in order that you may replace your sorrow with joy and your trepidation with love; to help you supplant separation with unity. You see, when you live in the Love state, not only are you in My Presence – it is there that you consciously merge with Me. But we have to get you there first, Dear One.

It may be difficult for you to understand that ...

I
Am
Here

communicating with you telepathically. But, at the very least, you cannot deny that we are having this talk, can you?

"You're right about that!"

But you are not the only one I am with. I talk and walk with everyone on every continent every day. It is just that many do not know how to recognize Me because they believe I am in Heaven, not on Earth. Then there are those who are completely satisfied with knowing that I exist, but care nothing whatsoever about doing the work required to see Me.

"Sometimes I can't even see You myself. I mean, I sometimes still buy into the belief that I'm having a relationship with others, not with You."

Yes, you still have a tendency to separate others from God. But not letting yourself see Me in others only brings grief and fear into play for you. The fact is, I am with everyone personally and directly all the time.

"So no matter what the scenario, even in an argument with someone else, I'm fighting You?"

Yes, it is true you are resisting Me, but you are really just fighting yourself. This is why an argument can never be won, because the fight is yours and yours alone. Has going against the grain ever worked for you?

"It sure hasn't. That's why I'm concentrating on learning how to stay in the present moment."

So now that you are living this way, do you find that things are changing for you?

"Yes, they are, and it's about time."

No, Keith, it is not about time, it is beyond time. I say again that you are eternal, sustained by the Word (Om). My great joy will be when you see just how beautiful you are, how vibrant, and how precious your life is to Me. When that day comes, you will discover within you the world, the cosmos – God, the One Life Force that permeates everything. Quite fascinating, is it not?

"I want that so badly and, yes, I'm very intrigued!"

Well, here is your chance, Beloved, because you are being blessed with the opportunity to achieve your potential by getting to know Me through you, as you. I want you to know that I find it a great privilege to know you through Me, as Me.

"What do I say to something like that except that I'm honored to be a part of Your message!"

Just to let you know, I have been trying to get your attention for a long, long time. Now, as you let yourself open, you will soon begin to see who I really am.

"I'll do my best."

I know how immense this challenge is for you because, since you were born, you have been instilled with the idea of separation. Because of this feeling, you have often forgotten your kinship with Me and that has caused you more grief in the long run than any dilemma you may have been confronting. But I bring you a love offering full of information to help you remember the peace you sometimes tend to overlook.

"I'm the first to admit that I need it."

On our spiritual excursion, we shall cover the basic principles that are imperative for your growth. We will first form a solid foundation of understanding so that we can then move onto firm footing to achieve the peace that you seek. Once you know yourself as a chip off My ol' block, you will then see how you have always had the power to create the best reality for yourself.

Thought energy is the primal force that gives birth to life in all its forms. Just because you are not aware of your thoughts after they leave your head, it does not mean that your thoughts die.

The moment you entertain any thought, the universe begins to work toward its manifestation. Everything is affected because all is One – the same Body, the same Being. For you to understand more fully that everything is of One Energy, we must start with the Soul and work our way outward.

Know that in every human being there are more bodies than

just the physical one, and there is much more taking place than meets the eye.

THE SPIRIT SELF OR BODY: The Spirit is the aspect that descends into a body to partake of the human experience. It creates and governs all that is you. The Spirit works in conjunction with your own awareness to bring about what is beneficial for your evolution so that you may one day embody the Divine Principle.

THE MENTAL SELF OR BODY: This aspect provides you with the ability to reason. What I mean by reason is having the capability to consciously recognize what is right for you in any situation. It is the part of you that creates by thought and choice.

THE EMOTIONAL SELF OR BODY: This aspect is denser than the spiritual and mental bodies and is responsible for physical expression. It influences all the actions and reactions triggered by your pleasure/pain memories. Its enormous power brings what you are choosing into the certainty of being.

THE PHYSICAL SELF OR BODY: This is what most people think they are – the body. But really, your physical body is just the vehicle for the other bodies. It lets you move freely in the world while you work to align your personality with your Soul. It is your individuality. Your physical self allows you to come together with others to share life experiences.

All these aspects make up the human entity. Even though they are different, they have one thing in common: they are all made up of energy. It is through such synergy that the physical, emotional and mental bodies connect to the all-pervading Spirit.

On the earth plane, almost everyone perceives himself or herself as an individualized unit, separate from others. Such spiritual deficiency promotes spiritual dyslexia – a view of reality as outer to inner, rather than inner to outer. This perception is in error because, at the subatomic level, there is no separation whatsoever. Everything is just energy fluxing at Godspeed, briefly bumping around, then off to somewhere else.

Believe it or not, the human body is 99.9999% empty space. The other .0001% (matter) is empty space as well. Matter consists of random blips of energy and informational discharges that solidify into a three-dimensional hologram, thus creating the illusion of solidity.

I know that grasping this concept has been challenging for you in the past, Keith. But are you finally beginning to see how everyone is of One Body that branches into many seemingly separate bodies upon the physical plane?

"Yes, I think I am."

The more you can see this truth, the more your tendency to judge anything will diminish because you will understand that everything is you. When you cast judgment, not only do you bring about division from others – you deepen the conscious breach between yourself and the One Cosmic Body. When you judge, love begins to decay and fear begins to expand.

Now, even though I describe separation as a truth in and of itself, in truth, it is not real. Nothing can ever leave My sight – that is the real truth. I live in such wholeness that I even hold together the things you may see as separate.

Here is an exercise for you. Look at your hand. Do you see it as a hand with separate fingers?

"Yes."

Because of those empty spaces you see between them, you think that one finger has no connection to the others. This is but a perception of separation caused by your lack of focus on the entire hand, which, after all, is where your fingers extend from in the first place. Your hand represents the place where all things connect and originate – God. This simple lesson should lift your awareness beyond any deception. Do you understand it?

"I've really gotta hand it to You. You've explained it so well that even I get it!" (slyly smiling)

Now let us look at the connection you have with the Earth and all the life upon it.

Again, I ask you to reflect on your body and see it as one living organism housing billions of cells – skin cells, liver cells, brain cells, blood cells and so on – all of them encapsulated in one wrapping of flesh.

This holds true for Earth as well, where there are billions of individual cells called people who differ from one another in personality, appearance, sex and race. Humans are embraced by a much larger organism – Earth. Humans are to Earth as cells are to humans. From micro to macro, the universal design is the same.

Atomic → Cellular → Body → World →
Solar → Galactic → Stellar → Universal

All systems spin around one central source. Atoms and cells have elements spinning around one central source called the nucleus; and you and Earth spin around one central source called the Sun. The solar system revolves around the Milky Way Galaxy with that huge star cluster at its center. Galaxies rotate around the cosmos, and the universe revolves around God – the Great Central Sun. I know you have heard the expression: "He thinks the world revolves around him." Well, this is the truth of it. Everything revolves around Me, for it is I who spins all into life.

"It sounds pretty simple, I mean, as far as how You've laid things out."

Yes, it is so simple that, without forcing anything, Truth brings about the natural flow of life and light that allows the Divine to be omnipresent. This is just the way it is! I do not judge it, for it is what it is.

"Do You think I'll ever get there in this lifetime?"

That is entirely up to you, Keith. Know that, even now, you have what it takes to grasp the complexity of the universe and to anchor the Divine Principle if you accept living in love as your abiding criterion.

With this new awareness of your relationship to Earth, other human beings and God, you now have the ability to understand all that is taking place in the era that you are living in. I share with you this truth of your connectedness to bring stability and to provide a deeper comprehension of how things will play out in these transitional times.

"You mean things will get worse before they get better?"

I did not say that, you did. But I can tell you that your unity with God and Earth will only aid you when the wheels of Spirit really begin to roll.

"That sounds both promising and ominous. What dynamic is taking place now?"

Earth's energy is beginning to shift dramatically and it is lifting at an exponential rate. The pace of life is accelerating like never before and in this age of computer technology, when new phenomena quickly become obsolete, most people find it tough just to keep up. But it is very important for all of you to update yourselves and absorb as much information as possible. After all, who do you think is behind this idea that you call the Information Age?

"That goes without saying."

Does it now?

"Well, it's obvious to me – You are!"

So why is the world so reluctant to use it to its fullest capacity?

"Ouch!"

Let Me put it this way: When humanity finally does get around to taking in what I have been saying for eons, world peace will be yours.

"So what should we call this time we're living in – the Beginning, the End, the New Age, the Golden Age, Revelation, Armageddon, the Rapture – what?"

It matters not to Me what you call it. What does matter is for you to believe with all you have that I am blanketing you and Earth with Love's vision so that humanity can see what has been created, how it is working and what needs to be recycled for your further expansion.

You must know that the "closer" I get to you, the more the Law of Cause and Effect will be in play. Said another way, as My Light pierces the illusion of time and space, everything about you will be unmasked to reveal your shadow self, your own illusion.

"Are You saying that cause and effect will not be separate and that our thoughts will suddenly begin to manifest?"

Right, kiddo! As the world keeps moving down its timeline, reality will indeed begin to immediately manifest from thought, because God-power is wending Its way through every Soul on the planet – making now the perfect time to manifest your own life's desires. But before we can truly work and play together, I must first mirror to each of you with all My Love exactly who you are as a think-ing, feel-ing, do-ing, be-ing being.

"So that's how the universe functions?"

Yes, absolutely. The whole system of Creation works in harmony, constantly learning and updating, ever expanding. And I am ready to reveal to all of you the progress we have made.

"So, if we're all partly responsible for creating this magnificent universe, why did any of us choose to consciously leave its grandeur and come to live on Earth?"

Just for the "hell" of it. Let Me ask you, are you having any fun?

"At this point in my life, I'd say I am – pretty much."

Well then, that is enough. We shall continue our discourse tomorrow.

How are you today, Keith?

"I'm just fine, thanks."

I am ready to transmit more information. Are you ready to transcribe it?

"I'm ready, but something's been bugging me all night."

I know. You have been wrestling with why I said, "Hell," yesterday.

"I didn't want people asking me a question that I didn't have the answer to."

Well, I can give you several of them.

First, I experience no guilt when I combine letters in a way that some call bad. You are the ones that react and your doing so last night just proves My point.

Second, I am only interested in results, and if using "hell" produces a desired one, then so be it. Anyway, Who do you think created all those dirty words you throw around?

Third, let Me answer your question with another question. You see what is going on; how do you think most people find life on Earth?

"I see Your point."

Let Me remind you that My existence is truly Divine. This implies that life for anyone not consciously connected to Me ...

"... can sometimes be hell. I get it."

The problem you are having is that you have gotten so wrapped up in the drama of life being just too much that you have forgotten to look to Me for relief. What I am trying to do here is unleash My Reality within you so that you can have your relief *and* your fun.

I am granting you awareness so that you can finish what we started and experience My Glory at a conscious level. All you need to do to be a conscious part of our great creation (and begin to have My kind of fun) is look within your own heart. In this readily available place is where you will find Me.

As I just illustrated above, all things in the universe are individual cells of God. As I embody you, you embody God. This is the sole/Soul reason you are here: to activate and anchor the Divine upon the Earth's physical plane.

"You may be having a blast on the cosmic level, but from

where I sit, things are not always so peachy."

Yes, you are right, Keith. From My point of view, I am on a fun-filled journey. I shall effort to make My utterances more down to Earth so that you can better understand and ultimately get to Heaven yourself.

"I'd appreciate that."

No problem.

There is enormous potential for unpleasant things to manifest in your life, but they need not necessarily come into being. You said it correctly: as Love energy continues to lift, things will quicken into manifestation. So if you wish to avert any adversity, you must clear yourself of any hate, guilt and fear you are holding on to. If these obstacles are not cleared, trouble will continue to show up for you on a regular basis.

It has been said that when the bad moon rises on people, God is testing them. This is completely nonsensical because such an assumption makes Me out to be the tempting devil that I most definitely am not.

It is ludicrous for people to think that I would tempt or tease them or play any part in their bad choices and the consequences that follow. When it comes down to the owning of a situation they may find themselves in, they want no part of it, so they play the "The devil made me do it!" card in a futile attempt to transfer their own response-ability onto a figment that does not exist.

These Divine/diabolical tests are given Soul→soul to generate experiences and to provide some Self↔self-reflection. I have no hand in such trivial matters. The fact that lessons come back around again and again only points out that people have not yet resolved specific negative energies.

But if you choose, Keith, you can own, integrate and transcend your own "stuff" and reunite with your Soul. Indeed, this reunion must take place before you can ever know God. But you see, Beloved, what you decide to do really does not matter to Me because, in the end (which, like the devil, does not exist), all creation will consciously return to Me. So why not go ahead and live your life with style, fun, joy and integrity – for these are some of Love's vital components.

"May I ask a couple of questions?"

That is one. (*chuckling*) Yes, of course, ask.

"What constitutes Love and can anything exceed the parameters of Love?"

The answers are very simple. First, if you do not use your free will to impinge upon someone else's, you are exercising My Love. Second, My Love knows no parameters. It transcends all boundaries of time, space and judgment. It adheres to no rules pertaining to this or that. I do not judge something to be anything other than Myself.

"But what I was taught ..."

Never mind what you were taught! I know this may not sound like the god you have been used to; nonetheless, these are the constructs of My Love.

"When trials show up in my life, does it mean that I've been abusing my free will? Is that why I sometimes feel You are testing me?"

I have never tested anyone. The truth is, you are testing yourself. Your unhappy experiences have come about because you have not yet worked through your karma. But if you wish Me to, I will test you here and now.

"No – not that!"

Relax, this will not hurt. (*laughing*)

"What do You have in mind?"

A test, like you had in school.

"But I did lousy in school. I failed a lot of classes. In fact, I didn't even graduate!"

Well, Beloved, My test is designed for you to pass! Do you not wish to put to rest the questions you are having about God, you and us, so you can get to a better understanding of the Law of One?

Just one note: for each question only one answer is possible – the correct one, the highest one. Prepare to earn an A+! The reward for your high grade is union. Know that you are so loved that failure is not an option. I await the moment when I place upon you that big gold star for scoring 100%.

Take a deep breath and relax. Ready?

"Yes."

Then we shall begin. Who am I?

"God."

Can God read your mind?

"Yes."

Would I not have to be somehow connected to you to do this?

"Yes, of course."

Is the mind of God clear?

"Yes."

Is there anything that I have created without clarity? If so, what do you think it would be?

"No, I don't think anything could've come about if You were not clear."

Is God a perfect Being?

"Yes."

Is God capable of creating anything that is not perfect?

"No."

Who created you?

"You."

Who created Earth?

"You."

Who created the solar system, which is one of infinity?

"You."

And Who created the Milky Way Galaxy, which is one of infinity?

"You."

Who created the universe?

"You did."

Who created God?

"No one."

And therefore ... ?

"You just are?"

Always have been and always will be. Who sustains your life?

"You."

Who sustains the life and movement of the solar system?

"You."

And Who sustains the life and movement of the Milky Way Galaxy?

"You."

Who sustains the life and movement of the universe?

"You do."

Again, Who sustains the life and movement of God?

"I can see now that everything – except You – is derived from You. So, I'm perplexed – what are You really?"

It would be more correct to ask what I am not, for there is no form that is not Me and there is no name that I do not bear. God is not My name, though the word does invoke an image of the Highest Authority. What I am is the Ultimate Awareness. What I am is Perpetual, Infinite Potential.

Surely you can understand that everything born of Infinite Potential has within it its own spark of Infinite Potential. Everything has infinite potential to become Infinite Potential. But to become invincible like Me, you must go deep within and reach for that Infinite Potential yourself.

"I think I may actually understand this!" (*amazed at himself*)

So you are not perplexed after all?

"No, I guess I'm not."

You see, by your intent to go within and seek, you have pierced your confusion at last. You have just become introduced to your own Infinite Potential. Now let us see what you do next.

As clearly as there are rewards for going within yourself for sustenance, there are definite consequences for going outside. When you reach out to grab the world, you are vulnerable to its influences and the rules that apply on the physical plane. It is there that you encounter the many distractions and temptations that result in your conscious disconnection.

Looking to the temporal world for what you think you need implies a belief that you are lacking something. I ask you, why must you reach outward for fulfillment? You can never reach your Infinite Potential and power that way.

"Hmmm ..." (*thinking about how often he reaches outward*)

Do you understand that God is Life Itself and is not separate from Creation?

"Yes, because if that were a possibility, all would cease to exist."

Seems to Me that you are getting the hang of it. The reason you and many sometimes find life so challenging is because you give credence to the idea that the world outside is something other than you. It is that which has caused so many of you to feel so alone. But – here is the kicker – all of you have the potential to tap into the Self that connects you to Me.

"Are You telling me that I'm just like You in every way?"

Let us say that you are already embodying many of My Principles.

"Like what?"

Like your innate ability to create a life of quality instead of one of mediocrity. As Scripture says: "You are created in the image and likeness of God." (Genesis 5:1)

"I used to think that that meant You thought me into being and made me to look kind of like You."

If you only knew how many people think that. (*laughing*)

"That is pretty darned funny." (*chuckling*)

But there is more truth inherent in this than first meets the eye. You yourself put it nicely just a moment ago: it means that you cannot separate from the things you have brought forth in your life, lest they cease to be.

To further My point, let us continue that test I was giving you to see what happens when you separate yourself from your creations.

What happens if you were to remove your life force (yourself) from your checking account?

"It's no longer my checking account. It closes."

What happens to a relationship when you break it off?

"It's no longer a relationship."

What happens if you decide to separate yourself from anything?

"I guess it would no longer be a part of my reality."

Do you find life filled with peace, joy, trust, love, compassion, acceptance, allowance, understanding, patience, and sharing?

"In many aspects of my life, I'm very happy. In others, there is definitely room for improvement."

Are you moving intentfully in that direction?

"Yes, I do my best to follow through, but I still procrastinate doing some things."

Why do you think you procrastinate?

"You're trying to tell me something here, aren't You?"

Yes, I am waiting to see if you dare do something about that habit of yours?

"This sounds like one of the traps I thought You were setting for me a couple of times before. But this time I don't want to be snared! By the way, didn't You say that You don't tempt?"

That is right, I do not. But, right now, you are the exception to that rule. (*picking on him*)

"You sound just like my dad!"

Yes. He picks on people he loves. Your father, he is a great and generous man. Oh, and let us not forget your mom who is the epitome of a Divine mother. She has to be to put up with the two of you! (*still teasing*)

"So that's how it's gonna be, huh?"

What do you say we call a truce and get back to where we left off?

"If I only had more time, I'm sure I could come up with a good one."

Well, I have all the time there is, so go ahead, give it your best shot! (*waiting*)

"Oh, forget it!"

What is the matter, Keith?

"I couldn't think of anything. You probably stopped all my incoming thoughts."

Yes, I do have the ability to do that. But I will send you some images if it will make you feel better.

"That was quick. I just got one."

Okay, let Me have it.

"What in Heaven's name were You thinking when You created the duck-billed platypus? I thought You were always clear!" (*laughing hard*)

Where did that come from? It was not Me that sent you that image!

"I have my ways of finding out what I need to know."

Got Me! So, do you feel better?

"Much! I'm ready to get back to work. Where did we leave off?"

Why do you think you procrastinate?

"You're still trying to tell me something here, aren't You?"

Yes, but this time I am waiting for you to tell Me how I can help you.

"Oh, I've got it! You're waiting for me to ask You for some help in letting go."

Ah, Beloved, just as I suspected, you are a good student!

Now, just a couple more questions.

If I am complete Love, is there anything I have created that is not an extension of My Self?

"Absolutely nothing!"

And, finally, if God is Love and you are God, why is fear a part of your experience and not a part of Mine?

"I have no earthly idea!" (*trying to be funny*)

I have to admit that is a good one, but not as good as the platypus!

Keith, fear is nothing more than that – a fear. Time and again, the mistakes that you have made by living without Divine Principles have perpetuated your fear cycle and have left you with all those feelings of lack. Remember, whenever you buy into one of your fears it is because you have a false sense of emptiness. I will break this down for you.

You can say that fear is ...

False
Emptiness
Actualizing
Reality

... a space void of Love – God – You. Fear is a self-created block that constricts you and keeps you from becoming open to the Divine Self that wants to pour through you and bring you fulfillment. So you see, even though you do have God qualities, fear is the one thing I do not share with you, for it has no connection at all to anything that is Love. The physics here should not be too complex to understand – fear is yours and yours alone.

Later on, when I share My Divine Principles and you begin to put them to use, you will see your fears dwindle. Living these Divine Principles will keep you focused on God as your only reality. Applying them at every opportunity will help you to become a part of the all-pervading reality of Love – the Living Truth.

"Sometimes it seems that, at the very time I'm feeling fearful, my fear is protecting me from something."

Does it seem as if it is protecting you from the very thing that you are afraid of?

"Yeah, that's exactly what it's like!"

What you have not yet realized is that your fear does not protect you. What it does is complicate the very scenarios you are efforting to simplify. You think that being afraid keeps you out of harm's way in a crisis, but what it does is throw you directly into its path where you must repeat the lesson, no matter how long it takes.

"So tell me, is reincarnation real and, if it is, is fear the reason I've had to do it so many times?"

Yes. According to universal law, all actions spawned from a fearful place must come back around for review and resolution. If you do not clear your present self of past problems, you will be reborn again and again until you do resolve them.

The thing I must tell you is that reincarnation both does and does not exist. When Scripture speaks of "the Beginning and the End," it is to accommodate your current frame of reference. Its concepts have to be conveyed in this way because, at this point, you are only mindful of a linear timeline and cannot easily conceive of eternity.

"Yeah, that's a tough one to fathom, alright!"

Well, try it now. Take few moments, Dear One, and meditate on eternity. When you are through, open your eyes.

"Okay, I'm done."

Tell Me, Dear One, how many Souls do you think there are? Take your time before you answer. Think about what you just experienced during your meditation.

"Um ... there's only one, but It has many facets."

Yes, and in eternity those many facets or faces of the One Universal Soul live all at once. So really, all there is *is* You (God). But your consciousness must flip-flop around and through the time-space continuum until you remember that.

Keith, you have lived many lifetimes only to find yourself here, now. Although you have lived in many different forms, none of them is what you are; for what you are is the Spirit that has lived, lives and will live forever.

"What have I done that has landed me in so many lives?"

In most of your incarnations you have chosen the world of the external and material over that of the spiritual, thus guaranteeing the repetition of your births and deaths.

But if you want to live eternally – where there are no more births and deaths, just life everlasting – you have to replace your fear with Love. Once you get to that level, your consciousness will no longer be interrupted, the cycle will no longer perpetuate. But, as of now, you are only the potential of what you can become.

"Whew, that's a lot to get!"

Yes, it is, My Friend, but I find I must often play with words to help you understand what I am conveying and, most especially, to enable you to grasp some inkling of the Wholeness that I am.

Look at the word:

E-X-T-E-R-N-A-L

Notice its similarity to the word:

E-T-E-R-N-A-L

Observe that there is just one difference: the "X" in the word eXternal crosses out and interrupts the flow of the word eternal.

This is exactly what happens to your consciousness when you choose to live in external mode. You cross out all your chances for eternity. And so the current of your life will go, until the time when you are able to live in unbroken flow. If you honestly seek union with Me, you must hold steadfastly to your intentions and be ever-vigilant. When you achieve this life-mode, then your next death cycle will be a Divine birth.

"Is that what it means to be reborn?"

Not quite, Dear Keith. Let Me be perfectly clear. Birth's intention is to not be born again and death's intention is to never again die. The intentions of both are the same – to give you every chance to consciously unify with All that is. Now, whether or not you choose to go along with this program is entirely up to you.

It is vital that you begin to inform yourself on all matters, especially spiritual teachings from around the world. When you do, you will find all the doctrines you study are but jigsaw puzzle pieces waiting to be assembled. And when the puzzle finally does piece together, do not be surprised to see the image of My Face shining through.

You must not accept blindly that everything you have been taught or will hear is true. Figure things out for yourself by weighing the possibilities and probabilities of what is the likely Truth.

"Is there anything You don't know?"

Ah, I thought you would never ask. Yes, there is one thing God is ignorant of – fear. Because there is no reality in such energy, I do not dwell there. Still, I see what fear does to all of you. It eats away at you like cancer. If you do not expose yourselves to My Love's radiation, fear will only continue to overtake your bodies. When it becomes too much, you will be forced to create your deaths to escape your unbearable lives.

Dear Ones, when will it dawn on you that wherever you go, you are still you! Nothing changes if you do not change yourselves from within, with or without a body. So I say to each of you, if you are sincerely seeking a better life, take responsibility and take action by pulling your perception out from under your fear. Only then will you be able to live in peace and share your love with all things in My Creation.

Now back to the basics of Self-love. It begins with finding the part of you that is original – your innermost Being – and consciously reuniting with It. Discovering such a sense of Self will introduce into your own life the same power to manifest that Jesus and other Ascended Masters throughout time have demonstrated in theirs. And it will bring you into balance so that the same Divine energies with which they created miracles will be available for your use.

Once you cross your spiritual threshold you will be able to further honor the contract that you made with Spirit before you were born, because you will then know through experience that the Life Force within you is God. You will have no choice but to live your life as a love offering. After all, this is your purpose, Dear One – to anchor the Divine Principle in your day-to-day reality.

"I'd love to be able to do that!"

What on Earth do you think you have been doing all this time?

"What do You mean?"

Are you not the one writing a book called *The Divine Principle: Anchoring Heaven On Earth*? And have you not been working on this daily?

"How did I not connect the two?"

Because you had not fully realized that you were having a talk with God! Now that you have chosen to open to the truth of who you are, you can become My channel. I could not have entered your consciousness any other way.

"Why wasn't I taught all this stuff when I was younger?" (*crossly*)

Well, did it ever occur to you that I might have been saving you? Believe Me when I tell you that your timing is perfect. Yes, Beloved, your Christ Self orchestrated this preordained path so that you would be ready to write My words at a time when they are needed most – now.

Besides, you have had some growing up to do. You have had to work through karma to learn, update and expand. And to your credit, you have taken these opportunities to begin to fall into alignment. All you have learned has not been in vain, My Friend.

"Thank You, I'm glad to hear that. But what about others? Why is alignment so difficult for them?"

Because most are still waging an ongoing war in their minds – that noisy battle between "right and wrong" – which has kept them rigidly locked in their "victim" position. Though you are now able to tune out much of your own mental static, know that most people have much more twisting of the dial to do before I can come in loud and clear for them too.

If one lives his/her whole life with a right/wrong point of view and uses past memories to handle present circumstances, the stillness and clarity necessary to make sound choices will never be available. I am not saying that that position is either right or wrong; I am saying it can only result in one of those two possible outcomes.

Ego keeps people strapped into the front car of their own emotional roller coaster on a ride that never ends, because just over every incline is another right/wrong scenario that launches them through those disorienting swoops and loops yet again. As long as people refuse to get off their judgment ride, they can never hope to plant their feet on the solid ground of peace.

Concepts of right and wrong are taught by and learned from parents, society and those who claim to be authorities on the subject of God's Word. But what if the true meaning of life is neither way? How on Earth can someone come to understand another alternative?

"Through a teacher who embodies it?"

Yes, I have sent many of them to the world to show you that there is a way that is neither right nor wrong. In a beautiful world, unconditional love would do the influencing, for it is the most effective way I know of to create the peace that you seek. Those who have not heeded these teachers' examples are living in a right/wrong world, which is why they have such trouble agreeing about what is supposedly right or wrong.

One way for you to get what I am saying is by observing life partners who claim to love unconditionally, but who remain stuck in their conditional condition, arguing all the time.

Another prime example is the strife that exists among many of the world's nations, each standing firm on "our idea is right" and "your idea is wrong." This attitude inevitably leads to arguments, wars and continued separation – frustrating standoffs between those who would rather defend their own position than concede and compromise.

Keith, you have tended to engage in this dynamic frequently, have you not? Am I "right" in saying that you have not achieved the effect that you were hoping for?

"Yeah, You're 'right' about both. But what about the people who say that their right or wrong opinion is based on God's Law?"

What about them? You are going to come across people, especially some religious leaders, who support that opinion by saying, "God has determined what is right and wrong, and God is something to fear!"

It never ceases to amaze Me when I hear fear and God in the same breath. The Scripture that says, "Judge not, lest ye be judged," does not mean that I judge your wrongs, then punish you for your "sins." It means that when you judge, you judge yourself for the poor decisions you have made in the past, and you judge others for the faults you see in yourself.

I am not like you in this regard. I have no past to cast judgment upon, for it takes all My time just to be the Love necessary to sustain Creation. My stance of unconditional Love defines Who I am!

What defines the world is its present dilemma – figuring out how to catch the ultimate wave of universal law. Up until now, most of you have wiped out in all your attempts because you have not yet learned the laws that will let you hang ten and master that ride all the way to Spirit. But now that I see your desire to change, I will present them to you. I will place you atop My surfboard so that you can finally coast in and land on My peaceful shore.

THE LAW OF GRAVITY: How is that for a law?

"That's a good one."

Until you are a master, if you go against this law, serious trouble is certain to come your way. Jumped off any buildings lately?

"No, and I don't intend to."

THE LAW OF KARMA: You reap what you sow. Cause and effect. This law ensures a Divine Order, and keeps it that way. Your difficulty has been that, until recently, you did not know that you are the one responsible for creating your reality.

THE LAW OF ALL POSSIBILITIES: One of My favorites. The universe is a place where miracles are normal occurrences and all things have a right to be. What will make everything possible for you is the clarity you find by pursuing God. But if you choose to keep on bearing the burden of doubt, the hopelessness that accompanies it will assure that nothing promising will ever come your way.

THE LAW OF GIVING: To give is to receive: the Way of Christ. Your illusion of lack has caused you to be selfish and to take, take, take, thus ensuring your ongoing impoverishment.

THE LAW OF PURPOSE OR DHARMA: Find what your own role is in My grand scheme and perform it by allowing your Spirit's expression to live and work in your life. Going against this law will put you on a sure path to misery.

THE LAW OF DETACHMENT: To find fulfillment in the indwelling God, all idol worship must be abandoned. Being attached to the external world does not work because when its temporal things are no longer a part of your life, your happiness most assuredly leaves with them.

Very simply, these are My Laws. If you work with them, they

will work for you. Ignore them and the simple becomes difficult. In a later chapter, I will offer even more guidelines for you to follow as you endeavor to live in Spirit.

"What about rules? Are there any?"

No. Just keep reflecting on what I said about The Law of Karma and that will keep you in order and eventually free you.

"Tell me again what's been binding me?"

Your mind. It is your prison and your ego is its warden! You stay locked up inside because you still listen to that keeper of fear and disregard My Laws. But from this day forth, you can pardon yourself from this life sentence by listening to Me and accepting the fact that

I

Am

Here

and I am offering you the key to unlock your Spirit. All you must do is accept it and know that you truly deserve all that is good. You must believe that the Christ is you and you must begin to live that belief so that you can marshal the power to move through the illusions of separation, disease and, ultimately, death that will continue to present themselves. Only your perception, there by choice, is what keeps you from doing that.

"Is there an original sin and, if so, what is it?"

That would be conscious separation from God. But conscious or not, you cannot separate from Me. And, despite your God-amnesia, your Higher Self remains ready to emerge so that you can become Love on Earth.

Another thing that keeps you from knowing the Self is the large dose of doubt you still carry from other lifetimes. When will you realize that doubt is a most destructive force to inflict upon yourself? What do you think prevents you from knowing?

"Confusion?"

Yes, but why are you confused?

"It's like there's a battle going on within me. I feel I know what's real, but my analytical mind still tries very hard to convince me otherwise. I guess I've allowed the stuff I've taken in since birth to rule all my decisions."

Yes, that internal struggle is what I meant earlier when I spoke about right and wrong. Confusion has shaped your every doubt; doubt has created your confusion and lack of clarity; fear has taken away your power to create the life you truly want. These are your only opponents. There are no others. The only way to win this game we are talking about is to stop playing it.

"How?"

Stop thinking that you yourself are incapable of creating something beautiful! When you doubt, you either move forward in time or back, away from the power of the here and now. Doubt always creates gravity, drag and dread, and, as soon as you entertain it, it stifles anything creative you are trying to will forth. Only when you trust that everything will fall into place, will you find real power.

"It's not that I don't trust. It's more that I don't know how to let go of doubt."

I know what you are trying to say, Dear One, so let Me suggest this:

Give yourself the gift of accepting – if only for a few minutes at a time at first – that you are in a state of knowing at all times, a state in which you can easily recognize whether or not there is doubt, whether or not there is trust, whether fear or Love is in charge of your life. Then begin to peg the power that doubt holds over you and use this to your advantage. If you notice doubt, just redirect your knowing to cancel it; realize that nothing can possibly manifest through it. Let the knowing part of you that so wants to blossom transform doubt into trust, then watch what happens. The knower within you, with the know-how to get you what you want, will silently emerge.

If you take your trust to the ultimate level (by wanting nothing and trusting your Higher Self – God – with your entire life), Spirit will begin to move within you and give you something far beyond what you can dream up on your own.

You have heard the saying, "It takes one to know one." In such a way, the Self will see Its own Beautiful Self – the True Miracle – for I am everywhere.

As you endeavor to see and be My Miracle, you will come across many keys that fit many doors. But only one will release you from the emptiness you feel.

"Which one is it?" (*knowing something's up*)

The one that opens the door leading to the void where miracles can happen.

"But it's so scary to go there!"

I know you feel intimidated, but I assure you that if you are willing to go through hell to get to Heaven, the Divine that occupies these seemingly empty spaces will be revealed to you.

"That's easy for You to say."

Know that I do understand your reluctance to confront the abyss of your own demons. That being said, do it anyway, for

I

Am

Here

with you, in places where you are not yet present with yourself, to give you what only I can – the feeling that everything is okay. All you need to do is let go and expand your awareness until you recognize the sureness of that.

"Will You walk with me?"

Right by your side, Beloved.

Now close your eyes and think of something that is really troubling you. Just breathe in and out evenly for a few minutes to fall deeper into yourself. Take notice of any of those negative feelings that come up. Then, with your last exhale, release your troublesome thought to the universe and listen carefully. Do you hear it?

"Hear what?"

The soft voice of the Soul whispering Its wisdom into your heart?

"I've been able to do this before when I've meditated on some other issues, but I can't seem to consciously make the connection on this one."

Then you must go even deeper within to discover where your demon dwells! When you find it, it will probably look like a scared child cowering in a corner. But do not be fooled by its appearance and do not attempt to offer it pity, because it can and will take advantage of you. If you must, use another intense visualization to yank your demon out of your subconscious, then offer it up to the Light of Consciousness and watch it melt like the vampires you have seen in the movies.

When you begin to see through all your illusions, the beauty that has always been there will humble you. The circle of life will then curve back within you and suddenly God will be present for you at a conscious level.

"What about my future lessons?"

When something happens that you know could potentially be with you for a long time, I suggest that you heed and heal it at the very moment it transpires.

"Please share with me how."

While an issue is new, it is still potential energy – it has not yet become static. But if you let it fester, it will put down deep roots in an effort to mire you in its illusion. The longer you/it stay/s frozen, the tougher the thaw will be.

I know that I have been telling you that everything is God, so you must be wondering how it is that "terrible" things can be God. What you perceive as terrible is not the reality of God, but an illusion created by you. What I am saying is that the mind can never open up enough to take God in, so you must open your heart in order to move out of any illusion and into My Reality.

"But how will I know when I'm there?"

You will know you are heart-centered when you begin to see a world made up of hues that you could never see before. Everything will appear different to you – as if illuminated. You will know you have become heart-centered when you notice that joy is residing within you full-time.

"That illumination thing's already happening a lot – where things seem to have that glow You've mentioned and everything looks like it's softly blending together. What I want to know is how to stay in that space longer."

I shall tell you how: Become conscious of keeping your breathing just as even and steady as you possibly can, not only when you are meditating, but all the time. When you begin to live your life with this relaxed, letting go kind of feeling and a willingness to lose everything to gain your Self, you will have joy and complete trust where there was none before, and that space you were looking to expand will do just that.

You must also stop reaching for other things first and then for God when it is convenient for you. Perhaps you have been trying to seek Me with all that wanting, but it is your idolatry that has actually kept you from My Bounty. Another thing that keeps you and all separate from Me and My Goodness is the very thought that you are separate, along with pondering the fearful thought that you are not. Need I remind you that you came here with nothing and you will leave with nothing? In the meantime, cultivate, nurture and develop your Soul – because that you can take with you wherever you go. And whenever your intent needs some adjusting, pull out your Bible and refer to this passage for guidance: "But seek ye first the Kingdom of God, and His Righteousness; and all things shall be added unto you." (Matthew 6:33)

Christ, Buddha, Krishna and many other Teachers have taught the message of unity with Spirit. And teachers still come, bearing the same message: Look within to know God. All of them say that the Profound cannot be found in a church nor in belief, but only in the temple of your heart.

"Would it be correct to say that the heart is a stargate?"

Yes, and when you traverse it, you will enter the Kingdom of Heaven where universal Love reigns. Once there, you will be overwhelmed by utter serenity. Meanwhile, daily meditation and prayer will help you to free yourself from the drag of time. Soon you will begin to feel much lighter because many obstacles that have made you stumble along your path will be cleared away.

"For sure I'll continue to meditate because I know my addictive personality and I know that if I hadn't found this path, I would've never been able to survive. I was playing way too many games and sometimes I still do."

I like games.

"Well, yes, but ..."

Loved One, if you wish to play a game – play the game that will spin you off the fear/time wheel once and for all! I cannot emphasize enough that you must always try to make your spiritual work fun, because having fun is what keeps you in that God state, totally unaware of time. Tell Me, when you are having fun, where does the time fly?

"Hey, it does seem to fly. Why's that?"

The bliss you feel causes time to disappear.

"Wow, that's really neat!"

Have you noticed how a heaviness often comes over you when you look at a watch or clock and realize there is something you feel you have to do that will take you away from your fun?

"Again, I ask, why?"

Because your conscious link to God gets broken when you do something you would not choose to do, but do anyway. That is when you move from eternal fun to dreaded time. When this happens, it only means that you have shifted from your heart to your head – from Love to fear.

I ask you, Keith, why would you not let God lighten your load, ease your earthly responsibilities?

"Habit?"

Can you be any more vague?

"Well, that's what comes to mind."

Here, let Me help you, Beloved.

You are having to work so hard because you still carry the feeling left over from your childhood that you are not good enough. You still think you must prove to others that you will come through in their times of need.

This is the kind of stuff that has blocked My Light from entering you. Hauling around these "having to do" burdens is why you still sometimes find yourself emotionally and physically exhausted. If you keep it up, it is your body that will pay in the end.

You must realize that you can serve Me in a far greater way than by trying to find love through approval. I need you, Loved One! Not to find love, but to be Love. This is your greatest responsibility. I promise that meeting it will be no burden on you and will benefit everyone. Until then, if you should ever feel overloaded, do the exercise you just learned. That will let you bring consciousness back into your heart.

Dearest, why wait to come to what you call "terms" with any aspect of your life? Why not let your heart's Rapid Response Team do the healing now?

"I guess my attempts to heal the present haven't worked because I'm so used to living from past to future."

No wonder. With your current way of looking at things, cause, then effect, is how you think it goes. But though you perceive the past and future to be completely different, I do not. In actuality, they are two sides of the same coin. Cause implies a past intention when measured against effect – the manifestation of that intention over a linear period. Thus, past and future have no choice but to be bridged by the eternal now, the wormhole that folds time and space. Believe Me, the moment you launch an intention, it is manifested!

As long as humanity is lost in time, all manifestations will seem to come as future occurrences. But as you release more fear, the time it takes for you to notice such manifestations will quicken. Only when you remove all doubt and mind clutter will you begin to assume mastership and be able to both manifest what you desire in a holy instant and anchor the Divine Principles for life.

"Does time have any benefits?"

Right now, the buffer of time is of great benefit, for if it were not for this shock absorber, the fear encapsulated in your head could not handle the events that might manifest immediately. Can you see why, in the afterlife, this is referred to as hell?

"Yes I can, because we exist in Spirit form there and cannot use time to act as our thought-buffer."

My, Keith, you catch on quickly! It is time that has fooled you into not knowing that you create your entire existence. The difference between you and Me is that you have been caught up in its illusion and bound to the body, so you cannot possibly see the next reality you have already created. Why? Your ever-active fear has denied you clarity and Self-love.

"Will You tell me more about what hell actually is?"

Yes, but I shall do that as we go along. For now, let us stick to the subject at hand.

When you unify with God, you become conscious of something so divinely laid out that struggle ceases to be an issue. You have only to think something, and bang! – it happens. This should give you some idea of the inexhaustible Love I have for you.

Many people remain unaware of how to create deliberately. But now that you are learning how, Keith, you can choose to not react to circumstance, but instead, put the power of Love into action to bring about what you desire and deserve.

Everything is there for you to understand, cultivate and grow from. Even so, to live "the good life," you must own every aspect of it. Only then can you begin to mend your personality that is split between pleasure and pain, good and bad, Love and fear. When you find your balance within the Divine dichotomy, your life will become one of Infinite Potential.

I ask you, has it not been rough living with this confusing split and not really knowing for certain who the heck you are?

"Oh God, yes! Sometimes it's been too much to bear."

In your earlier years, you tried to be a "good" Christian by ignoring your darker side; but this did not work for you because all your untended-to fears were left to grow wild like weeds. When they got thick enough, they started to leech vital, nourishing energy that could have been used for your enlightened growth. Dearest, you have cut those weeds down quite a few times by doing productive things. But because you have not yanked all of them out by their roots, over time they have regenerated and have caused you even more grief. That is why the results they have produced have been neither permanent nor absolute.

Some of your forgotten fears are still mani-festering in your subconscious – inactive, but so very active. Because of your well-intentioned attempts, you sometimes think they are gone, but they are not. And as long as you continue to neglect them, the energy flow within you will continue to be obstructed.

Now do you think you know the answer to the question, "If I'm a good person, why do all these 'bad' things happen?"

"Yes."

Even so, I still see you and others pray to many deities when you are troubled. Sometimes you must wonder if your prayers are heard.

"Well, are they?"

Beloved, you know better than to ask that.

"Yeah, I do. But why is it that sometimes we don't get what we ask for?"

You always get what you ask for! No prayer remains unanswered, though sometimes it may seem to be that way. Even a prayer that comes from lack is answered and, since lack can only beget lack, if you ask Spirit to help you to be irresponsible, then so be it. If you expect any deity to unburden your troubled souls, you will all be waiting for a long time. Why should anyone other than you assume your responsibility?

"I don't know. Why?"

Because My system is not designed to work any other way. Because the Lord helps those who help themselves. Because Heaven on Earth cannot be anchored until everyone assumes My kind of responsibility!

Now is the time to assess your self/Self in a way that you have not done before. Believe Me, denial is not that river in Egypt. Denial only creates piles of confusion, kind of like the dog poop you inevitably step in because you do not see it. To help yourself out of the mess you are in, you must wear responsible shoes and walk responsibly in them. Responsibility only comes when you embrace your entire Self, fears and all.

"I wish I could just throw all my fears in the trash can."

If you could, along with that toss would go the wisdom that shapes you, for both are parts of your perfect design. And besides, if you did not have the fears you have, you would be someone else.

What you can do is change what fear means to you. See it as a tool to help unfold the wisdom you have within. You are the Dreamer, your own Creator Almighty; and yes, Keith, it is you who have been making this up for a very long time – in fact, for an eternity!

I am pleased to tell you that you are getting much better at the "making up" process. I see you manifesting reality with effortless ease in your sleep states of consciousness, and I know that your goal is to be able to do this in the waking world. But because of your repeated mistakes, you have been stuck in time – trapped between realms. The truth is, you are in perfect placement to get to the other side of stuck, which is freedom. You are close – so close!

"What do I do to keep getting closer?"

Again, call a meeting with the two aspects of your self/Self and have a healing session. Go inside and embrace your pain, invite it, feel it, then change what it means to you by recognizing from your heart's perspective the beauty of your predicament.

"What do You mean by 'the beauty of my predicament'?"

That I am with you every moment, just waiting to give you the gift of your True Self. Dear One, you must do as you have done before and ask, "God, where are You in the illusion that overwhelms me?" Then step outside of it and watch Me go to work on your situation. But stay aware of My every move so you will know when it is time for you to step back in.

It gives Me immense joy to be consciously recognized by you – the very same joy you get when you know that you are recognized by Me. This is how you anchor Me within you and come aboard the Good Ship Homeward Bound.

Keith, I see you as a slumbering aspect of Myself. So, as your Loving Parent, I say to you, "Hey, sleepyhead, are you not ready to get up and start your eternal day?" My Divine Child, awaken and use your God-given instincts as your guide. Your whole life awaits!

"What do You mean by instinct and where does it come from?"

Instinct is life's common thread of knowing and purpose. It comes from all previous times to guide you on the right path – the path to Spirit.

"I see."

It is not enough to see. You must look! "And ye shall seek Me, and find Me, when ye shall search for Me with all your heart."

(Jeremiah 29:13–14)

To All My Children: For the world to attain Heaven on Earth, things cannot be as they are now. It will take all nationalities coming together to achieve the goal of love, peace and unity. Trust that I will guide you in whatever you do. Just remember to breathe and do your very best to live in Love, give in Love, be in Love – and Love you shall receive! It is time to embrace yourselves, embrace all of humanity and embrace the Earth. Do this and you embrace God. Join Me!

Integration

Dreams, Dreams, Dreams

Whenever I do presentations about The Divine Principle: Anchoring Heaven On Earth, *I tell the audience, "Before I 'heard' God's Voice that one day, in June of 1996, I never saw 'It' coming. After the experience, when I was able to see more clearly, I knew my encounter with the Divine was destined to happen at some point in my life." That would definitely explain the passion I have to write books, create music and make movies that help others follow their own script leading them to a life of bliss.*

As far back as I can remember, I had great passion and sincerity about everything I did, and because of it, I've witnessed its amazing manifesting power. Not only has it brought me everything I've ever wanted in life but brought God as well!

Passion and sincerity do not discriminate. When people are angry, mistrusting, afraid or jealous, with the same kind of oomph I use to create a life of goodness, the Creator will grant them whatever it is they are asking for all the same. "For the Love of God! Why in the world would God give me all that unpleasant stuff?" you may ask. Because an Unconditional Parent doesn't know any other way to be; it's in the design of Its very existence.

It's obvious to me that the Creator of All That is Good knows nothing of sickness, lack, worry and fear, giving It the freedom to do what It wants – create – and create through us. So, it's my hope one day you will understand that whatever lies inside of you gets projected onto the screen we call reality.

Like it or not, conscious or not, day in and day out, we are constantly asking Source to, "Please give me an abundance of this or that," just by being who we are. It's not about formal prayer. It's about the language we are most fluent in – vibration! So, if nothing ever changes in your life, it is because you haven't changed. It's all God's unconditional Love, for your sake.

Though I didn't know it at the time, Sai Baba began to come to me in sleep states of consciousness in early 1997. At first, He'd come in different forms; probably to acclimate me to His slowly but surely, ongoing and frequent presence.

For instance, on a few occasions, before I ever heard of Sathya Sai Baba, He came to me in my dreams often as the spiritual author, Deepak Chopra. Although it was Baba, my mind could not register an unknown face and selected the nearest likeness. If one were to look at a picture of Dr. Chopra and Sai Baba, my point would be understood. Not only do they look a lot alike, they represent the same spirituality. And, I know it was Baba because of the dialog that transpired during these visits.

I want to share with you that my experiences with Sathya Sai Baba are not ordinary dreams. It's nothing at all like watching a movie on the mental screen and not being able to interact. When these visits happen, I'm just as aware as I am in my waking state – sometimes more so. And, I now realize that the reason I'm so present when He comes to me is because of my passion to follow Him and His teachings.

Sai Baba has a way of doing things that are not like any teacher I've known. Throughout all of the books I've read about His life, everyone who has actually met with Him said the same thing, "You cannot dream of Baba. If you see Him in this state, it's an actual visit done by His will." I speculate that this is why we don't dream about Jesus, Buddha or any other deity. If you could, everyone would be saying that their chosen Lord had visited them and told them this or that. So, remember, if you ever have an experience with one of these beings of Higher Consciousness, count your blessings!

The first time I saw Sai Baba as Himself in a dream was in late 1997, where I was standing in someone's front yard participating in a garage sale. After a few moments into the experience, a beautiful, white Rolls Royce drove up and parked alongside the curb. Once the engine was turned off, the chauffeur got out of the car and slowly opened the door for the backseat passenger. Out stepped a barefooted little man clad in an orange robe. To my amazement, it was Sai Baba, the Teacher I longed to be with.

Baba began to walk around the yard looking at all the items that were for sale. There were tables, lamps, books and knickknacks of all sorts spilling out of boxes. Wanting to get as close as I could, I began to follow Him through the maze of sale items no longer useful to its owners. I feel that this was a metaphor for me to follow the Leader and live my life by His example.

One night, I thought of calling my then girlfriend, Wendy, to see if she wanted to come over and hang out. But, as I picked up my phone, I decided to put it back down, somehow knowing that she would stop by without me even asking. Right then and there, "Knock, knock!" was the sound that filled the air, my ears and heart. I opened the door only to see Wendy standing there with a big grin on her face.

"Oh, my God!" I thought, seeing how we were wearing the same thing: aqua-blue tops, black sweatpants and white, striped ankle socks.

As soon as she walked in and sat down, I began to share with her the dream experience I had with Sai Baba. The whole time I was telling her about it, I could see that she was flipping out and couldn't wait to tell me something. When I was finished, Wendy immediately began to share a dream she had with Baba on the same night that included a vision about my future. This is what she told me.

"Keith, in the experience, Sai Baba manifested two rings."

"Really?" I replied.

"But there is more that happened. Let me finish!" she said. "I was sitting on this very couch next to Sai Baba when He induced a premonition of you going to India. In my vision I saw Baba coming out of His room and there were lots of people sitting on the ground. Baba walked over to you and put His hand on your shoulder saying, 'I will see you tonight.'

I also saw you lying down on a bed meditating or sleeping while you were in India, and that Sai Baba was going to appear to you while you were doing so. And as you were to fall asleep, He was going to share with you something of great importance about a prophetic event."

All I could say was, "Wow!"

Wendy and I had a good and fun relationship, but it only lasted a few more weeks from that point. I was single for about six months when I met and began to date someone by the name of Shannon.

One night when Shannon and I were hanging at my apartment, she told that she had a very strange dream and wanted to know if she could share it with me.

I said, "Sure."

She told me that she found herself conscious of my bedroom, when all of a sudden, what she believed to be a powerful spiritual being came in the room and laid down next to her. As she got her wits about what might be happening, the being sat on top of her and began to morph itself to look like me. I absolutely believe this was done by the being to form a level of trust so that she could relax and open up to the experience.

Then the being began to look in Shannon's eyes, asking her telepathically if she could hear it. After affirming, "Yes," the being gave her this message: "Tell your boyfriend, Keith, that he is not yet ready. But when he is complete, he will follow."

At this point, the being moved the altar I had in my room, from up against the wall, onto the bed using his spiritual powers for her to see – indeed, reinforcing that it was of great significance. Shannon then told me that she believed it was Sai Baba.

As I continued to study Sai Baba's teachings, it wasn't uncommon for me to fall into prayer and ask Him for His help to achieve all the things I wanted. One of those things was for Him to keep coming to me in my dreams.

The second time I'd seen Sai Baba in a dream I was floating in the sky and surrounded by light. When out of nowhere, He appeared next to me and asked, "What is it you want, Keith?" So elated with His presence, I couldn't speak. He said to me, "What you long to do, my son, is fly!" and off we went at Godspeed into many dimensions of light.

The third time I saw Baba in a dream was in a baseball stadium. When I came to a conscious state, I noticed someone standing next to me in the hallway holding a book titled *Universal Leela* (Divine sport or play). While waiting there until the game started, in walked Sai Baba. He came up to me and told me to open my right hand. When I did, there appeared a small book with the word "Record" on it that was embossed out of my skin. He then told me to close my hand and look again. That's when I noticed the word "Record" had morphed into the word "Life." He then said goodbye and walked to the bleachers to sit and watch the game.

When I woke up the next morning, I immediately began to interpret the experience and realized what He was conveying to me. That is, "When you begin to 'Record' words and music for Spirit, you will have 'Life' in the palm of your hand and that is what will lead you to everything you have ever wanted."

In my fourth dream experience with Baba, we were face-to-face. When He looked at me, I found it difficult to hold my focus, probably because I was afraid that He might "see me" in all my folly. But, when I finally mustered the courage to look into His eyes, they were all pupils that suddenly changed into twinkling stars. Right then, I knew the universe was contained within them. He smiled pleasantly and said, "Soon, I will come back." It's always uplifting for me to have an experience with this Master who comes to love, teach and nurture me towards an expanded consciousness such as His.

From that point forward, I had more glimpses of Baba in my

dreams, but it wasn't until late 1998 when they began to happen in a big way.

One night, I was out in dreamland when I had an experience with Baba that filled me with utter bliss. I was standing in a field with two other people; Baba was looking at us from a distance. After pointing to the person on my left, Sai Baba turned His hand and materialized a small ball of light. He then threw it at the guy, hitting him in the heart and knocking him to the ground. The young man, now in a fetal position, started to tremble and mumble. I had no earthly idea what was happening to him.

The next thing I knew, Sai Baba pointed at me and started to turn His hand, insinuating that I was next. *"Oh, oh! What's this?"* He then threw a ball of light at my heart and I also fell in a fetal position alongside the guy to my left. When this happened, I was filled with probably the most bliss I've ever felt in my life to that point. The same thing was done to the lady who was standing to my right.

As we all three lay there on the ground shaking from such intense bliss, Sai Baba came over and began to wave His hands through the young man's body and talk in a language I didn't understand. The guy started to react very strangely. As Baba did the same to me, He said, "Keith, what I am doing will take you to another level of feeling altogether." He then proceeded to wave His hands through my body and speak in that same language. I have no idea what happened to the lady on my right after that because I jetted off to another level of consciousness.

In this new dimension, I found myself in a field cradled in Baba's arms, as if I were a baby in a grandparent's care. There were people all around us, and my guess is that they were there to witness what was to happen next.

Sai Baba looked to me and said, "Keith, would you be willing to go wait outside of your apartment in the parking lot all day this coming Tuesday? If you do this, I will pick you up and take you to India for two weeks. Would you do this for Me?"

With tears in my eyes then and as I write these words now, my comment to Him was, "I would do anything for You!"

Tuesday morning, I woke up with the joy and excitement of knowing this could be more real than I ever thought possible, so I didn't hesitate for a moment. I got up, dressed myself in shorts, tank top and sandals and headed out the door. Once I got to the parking lot, I found a curb to sit on thinking, "This looks like as good of a place as any. Now, all I have to do is wait … and wait … and wait."

One hour rolled by and the July sun was getting hotter. Sitting there in the heat, I began to wonder, "What in the world am I doing out here? I wonder if He's ever going to show up." After a few minutes of deliberating, I began to realize how this might be one of those times when Baba was playing with me. From my ongoing interactions with Him, I knew the possibility and the likeliness of that being the case.

After a few more minutes of pondering and sweating like no tomorrow, the idea became clear to me that He was toying with me to see how devoted I am to my growth. "This has to be a metaphor for something else." But then again, I read many stories where Sai Baba had performed miracles that would make this curb sitting and waiting to go to India seem like no big deal.

For a while longer, I continued to go back and forth from my mind to my heart looking for an answer. At noon, I decided I'd had enough and headed back upstairs to my apartment into the cool air.

Later that night as I lay in bed thinking about the day, my mind started up again and brought me to the point that I felt a break inside. I was so pissed at myself. Heat or no heat, I should've never left that curb! That kind of devotion is what brought Siddhārtha Gautama His awakening. After many years of searching for God, Siddhārtha sat under a Bodhi Tree where He vowed, "I will sit under this tree until I become enlightened." The next morning, when He saw the sun rise in all of its beauty,

Siddhārtha Gautama became the Buddha.

Even though I didn't follow through with sitting on the curb, I began to see how my wishing I did and actually doing it was professing the same love for God whether I waited or realized. A week later, I had the most profound dream with Sai Baba to that point.

It started with Baba standing on the shore across a river. When He noticed that I saw Him, He began to speak to me telepathically saying, "Keith, you and your friend, Mike, should come to see Me in India." Mike is the person I mentioned in the last chapter and the one who put me the spiritual path to awakening.

Although Baba's words in this dream were few, the impression spoke volumes. It was a feeling ... a knowing ... a premonition ... a vision.

"How will I get there? Where will I get the money to be able to go? How do I put all this together? How long should I stay?" I asked Baba.

"Keith, you have to learn to transcend your doubt and disbelief. If you come here just to put your feet on Indian soil only to turn around and go home, this is what you should do," said Baba.

I woke up that morning trying to figure out if my experience was meant for me to take literally or not as before in the parking lot. Back into my head I went ... *"How do I go about making such a journey happen? Where will I get the money to do this? When should I go? How will I get there?"*

Then it dawned on me, *"If God invited me to come to Him, any logic would have no bearing whatsoever and everything will unfold on its own. All I have to do is be aware of Spirit moving and follow the signs that would begin to present themselves."*

That day, about noon, just to see what would happen, I called Mike and asked him if he'd be interested in making a trip to India with me. He said that he was up for it, but wanted to know what prompted me to want to go. I told him what had happened just hours before. He laughed and said, "Guy, it sounds like a lot of fun!" For the rest of our conversation, Mike and I started to lay the groundwork for our possible pilgrimage.

Two weeks had passed as I constantly entertained the possibility that I might at long last be with my Teacher and washed in His Presence. Just when I thought my spirits couldn't get any higher, the phone rang.

"Hello?" I answered.

"Hi, Keith, my name is Debbie. We have a dear, mutual friend by the name of Nadhim. He told me that you are planning a trip to India, but was not sure how you were going to get there. So, I felt compelled to call you and help you out," she told me.

"What do you mean?" I asked.

"Mr. Blanchard, I am a flight attendant, and every year I am given buddy passes for my own personal use. But, if I don't use them, I can't carry them over into the next semester. I thought you should have one for your trip to see your holy man," she said.

I freakin' hit the floor! I cried, cried and cried with such immense joy that I called everyone I could think of to tell them of the miracle that had just taken place in my life.

Over the next couple weeks, Mike and I began to carry out our plan to go to India to see Baba. We came up with a date in late November which was only two and a half months away. With our departure fast approaching, I knew I'd better get things moving and in order, like saving money, finding a pet sitter, getting a visa, getting a passport and much more.

A month and a half went by when I got a call from Mike with some not-so-good news. He told me the target date we had chosen was not good for him and that we would have to postpone the trip. Sad, but knowing everything was in order, we shot for a date in mid-December. Once again, we were back on track, just waiting for the twelfth month to roll around.

The beginning of September, I met Kimmie. She was a

waitress at one of the clubs I played every Sunday named Willie Moffatt's. One night, I mentioned to her all that was going on with me and Sai Baba. She told me that she knew of Him and even had a book about His life. We talked for hours about what each of us thought to be spiritual "truth" as well as Baba's role in it.

After a few months of dating, Kimmie brought to my attention that she wanted us to start thinking about the idea of taking our relationship more seriously. I told her I was okay with it, and that we could talk about it more when I returned from India. I knew I had to keep my focus on the journey there for the time being.

The next day, I visited some very nice people who ran the Sathya Sai Baba organization here in Memphis, Tennessee. After being there a short time, I told them of the dreams I had with Baba and that I was going to see Him soon. You should've seen everyone's eyes that heard what I had to say.

Just then, the man of the house told me how lucky I was that Sai Baba awarded me the grace to personally experience Him and His Divinity. He also told me that, though many are drawn to Baba, the ones He comes to personally and invites are likely to be granted an interview. I thought, *"Wow! How awesome that would be to have a one-on-one with God in the physical way."*

One thing was for sure, not only was I excited about what I stood to gain from my journey to India, but what I would release to unburden my soul that would allow me to live in the Light again.

In the week that followed, I was told by an intuitive friend that, when I got to India, I was going to receive some kind of honor from Sai Baba. *"What honor could I possibly receive? Was I that 'good'? Did I do something in this life or a past one that deserves reward?"*

Understand that when I share things of this nature with you, it's not done with a sense of specialness. It's more to tell you of everything that happened so that even I could discover what it meant in its true context.

As soon as I left the Sai Baba Center and got in my truck to go back home, a profound thought from Baba came to me. "This is your journey, Keith, and maybe the honor is all Mine, and in this moment that is what you are receiving, My honor. Although I may have more to grant you when you come to India, I wanted to give you a glimpse into the grace that is coming because of your devotion to Me."

You see? That's what I'm talking about. How Creator, God, Jesus, Sai Baba, Buddha, or Whoever, will come into your life when you make yourself available, and with such a punch of light that there's no way you can deny Their omnipresence. Thank you, Lord!

About a week later, I went back to the Sai Baba Center for a meeting about how to prepare for my journey to India. Before I left to go home, I asked the man of the house if he knew where I could get some of the ash that Baba creates because I was out. He said, "Yes!" and then handed me a packet of it. When I asked him where he'd acquired this from, he said, "Follow me."

The man then led me to a shrine he had in his house devoted to Baba. When I walked in, there was an amazing and beautiful energy that permeated the entire room.

He told me (while pointing), "There ... that's where I got the ash I just gave you." Lo' and behold ... the mother lode! I couldn't believe my eyes. There was a large picture of Baba with the ash spontaneously falling from it. There was so much ash that the altar below and the figurines that sat on it were almost completely covered.

"How long has that been happening?" I asked.

"This has been going on nonstop for a few years," he replied.

When I got home from my trip to the Center, I walked over to my altar and picked up the bowl to refill it. When I removed the lid, I saw that the bowl had already been filled to the top. I know there wasn't any ash in there before, as to why I asked my friends if I could get a pinch of it in the first place. I remember wiping the bowl clean with my finger to get the very last of it to use in a meditation. This miracle is nothing new. Followers of Sai Baba have reported these kinds of manifestations for years.

Just days after going home to find my bowl refilled, Kimmie came to my apartment for a visit. After she got settled, I told her what happened with the vibhuti ash suddenly appearing a few days before. Amazed at the miracle, she excitedly went on to tell me about a dream that she just had with Sai Baba.

She told me that Baba came to her telling her things that were personal, but also manifested two rings; one for her and one for me. Of course, this seems to correlate to the two rings Baba manifested for Wendy in her dream. Was Wendy foreseeing a possible future for Kimmie and I?

November 23rd, Sai Baba's birthday, I got another call from Mike with more not-so-good news, telling me he couldn't do the trip in December either. The earliest he could make it would be February. My heart fell out of my chest as if my best friend had died. I was so heartbroken, and didn't know what to do, or if I was ever going to see Sai Baba. I found myself wanting to throw in the towel to this whole India thing.

It was in my last whimper that a profound thought hit me like a ton of bricks. *"Mike and I are to go to India to see Baba, but not together!"* When I realized that this was the way it was supposed to happen, I started jumping up and down, saying out loud, "I'm going to India!" the same way a child would who had just been told they are going to Disneyland.

Knowing that Mike and I were to go to see Sai Baba separately, I went about telling friends of my pilgrimage and how I was going alone. One such friend I told was a person named Mike S.

"Why would you ever go alone? Would you like some company?" he asked.

"Sure!"

I thought to myself, *"Maybe this is the Mike that was supposed to go with me."* But, why did it seem so clear to me that it was supposed to be the other Mike? Mike S. and I started making plans and began to lay down our journey.

Just when things were beginning to look good for our trip, Mike's side of things began to fall apart. He had an illness in his family and his presence was needed. So, I found myself once again a loner and somewhat puzzled about Baba's invitation for one of the Mikes and me to come to Him. I decided to release it all and just be happy that I was going.

Finally, it all began to make sense – *"Everyone's path to higher consciousness is between that person and God and no one else."* The feelings that started to well up inside of me were so fulfilling that I truly felt alive for the very first time in my life.

By the time late December rolled around, I had just about everything I needed for my trip: passport, visa, flight times, and all the money to have fun. I asked myself, *"Is there anything I'm overlooking? Maybe I should buy a tape recorder to log my thoughts so I could write a book about my sojourn and the play of Baba in my life. Yeah ... that's what I'll do!"*

That night I had a dream experience with Baba where He manifested two identical rings with hearts on them and placed them in the palm of my hand. At the time, I believed that it represented my unity with Spirit. But now, years later, I know without a doubt these rings meant that I would one day be married to my second wife, Kimmie. The fact that these rings were the same was showing me how a second chance to be in harmony or heart-to-heart (like on the rings) with someone would happen.

Still in the dream sequence with Baba, I asked Him if He would please manifest some holy ash for me. He said, "Why don't you do it yourself, Keith?" So, I turned my hand round and round as He does, and out pours ash from mine into His.

The next morning, as I thought about my trip to India, I

reminded myself to go with no expectations, except to come back fully charged and illumined. But yet, I kept getting the impression that Sai Baba was showing me things *to* expect through the visions I was having. I wasn't sure; maybe it was just my ego twisting things around inside hoping I'd get what I wanted.

I asked myself if given the chance, *"What would I want from Baba if I could have it when I get to India? I would love for Him to manifest a real ring with sacred writing on it as a million others would like."*

Although it was a want, it didn't consume me. But what I didn't understand was why there were so many dreams and experiences taking place that pertained to rings. For example: One day, I was sitting on the couch about to take off a pinkie ring I often wore to give my finger a chance to breathe, and as I looked at my hand, I noticed that I didn't have it on. But I swear I could feel a ring on my finger that day as to why I had wanted to take it off in the first place. I remember thinking, *"What in the world? When did I take it off? That's strange! What's the deal with rings?"*

The many times I'd been hanging out with Baba in my sleep experiences, I seen Him in kind, supportive, happy moods. When I first saw Him on one particular night, I was so excited that I cried. But what threw me for a loop was when He told me, "Stop your damn crying!" then turned His back on me and walked away. I knew immediately why He did that.

For quite some time I'd been praying for His help to conquer some of my vices and addictions to this world and did nothing to see it through. I was being a hypocrite and saw it so clearly. Turning His back as He did was telling me to not waste His time and to grow up. When I awoke the next morning, I felt ashamed and disappointed in myself. What a reality check!

A few nights later I had another encounter with Sai Baba. I was in India walking around when I saw Him in the distance, and as before, I started to follow Him wherever He went. Every time I got close to Him, He turned a corner. I was sure then He was toying with me so that I could see how badly I wanted to be with Him, only to understand now that He was trying to get me to really like being with myself. That was His way to have me stop relying on Him as my sustenance and look deeper within.

When I finally caught up with Baba, we were in a small room decorated in a Hindu motif. He asked me to remove my shirt. Without hesitation, it was off. He then asked if I would tear it into strips and join Him on the floor. After ripping the shirt from top to bottom into long, neat pieces, I lowered myself onto the floor and found a baby elephant lying on its side. I had the feeling that this was Baba's pet, Gita, that I read about in books.

The story of Sai Baba and His pet is very beautiful. Their love for each other is so great that Gita literally cries whenever Baba leaves after a visit. It's also told Gita's so evolved that, in her next incarnation, she will be born human.

Back to the dream.

After I finished ripping my T-shirt into pieces and joining the two of them on the floor, I began to wonder if the elephant was injured, assuming that the cloth would be used as gauze. Reading my mind, Baba told me, "Yes, it does look like gauze, doesn't it?" He then smiled.

Looking to Gita with the intentions of administering aid, I realized the elephant was not hurt whatsoever, but was just born. I immediately thought, *"This must mean a new birth for me."*

Two nights later, in another dream, when I came to a state of consciousness, I found myself running as fast as I could from a monster that was chasing me. When it all became too intense, Baba pulled me out of the illusion and placed me on the couch in my apartment where He sat next to me. He then got up and left me alone to stabilize from the panic of being chased by a large, horrible creature. No sooner than I started to calm down, Baba reached over from behind, tapped me on the leg and said, "I will be with you in a moment. I have some things to take care of."

After a while, Baba returned and told me that He was ready for me. I blacked out for a moment and became conscious of another room with Him sitting directly in front of me. I could feel His breath on my face as He began to speak. "I saw you, Keith. Boy, you have got some imagination. It's so big! Where do you create these creatures from?"

After we laughed for a bit, Sai Baba told me, "You are one fortunate individual! I am granting you something that only few will ever have. I will give you an interview (inner view). I do not give these out like candy, you know." I felt so blessed.

"Tell me about my life, what's my purpose here on the Earth?" I asked, dying to know.

"You are here to write songs, for they are all around you – new ones, old ones – pull them out and do something with them, because this is what you should be doing," He shared with me, further revealing my Divine Script.

After Baba told me about my purpose, I immediately thought to myself, *My God! This Being knows everything I've done,"* along with feeling shameful about some of the choices I'd made in my life.

While I was sitting there sulking in my self-judgment, I began to feel very heavy. So much so that I became aware of gravity and its pull on me. Baba was not going to stand for that! He was not judging me, and by God, He was not going to let me judge myself either. Baba then put His hand under my chin and raised my head as He made a weird monkey face and said, "Booga, booga, booga, boo! Lighten up, Keith, everything's okay," cracking up in laughter. Needless to say, the gravity that weighed so heavy on me began to lift and I felt much better. He then nodded to me, implying that the interview session was over.

I asked Him, "One more thing, please?"

"Sure," He said.

"There are some things in my life I need help with."

He then reached over to touch me on my face and I could actually feel it. "Good enough," He replied, as He pointed to a man standing in the corner as if awaiting instructions.

"Keith, this is My personal assistant. You are going to be here for a number of days; make yourself comfortable, for I have some things I must attend to. My attendant will get you whatever you need. Again, make yourself comfortable."

I love writing books! I can tell you that the first one was not only therapy for me, but also a great journey filled with fun and joy. I feel that in those eight years of searching inwardly, I've accomplished a lot, shaving miles off my trip homeward into becoming a conscious being.

Another thing about writing books is that I really love throwing around possible book titles, because it gives me an idea of the direction the work might take. Depending on which name I lean into at any given moment, it also seems to help establish a certain tone. From there, I may go to another potential title to try a new tone or feel altogether.

I get such an amazing feeling whenever I see a new book I'm writing begin to take shape and resemble a finished work. Even now, writing this one, I can feel a rush of energy come in just thinking about holding the first printed copy in my hands.

One night in a dream with Baba, I could feel Him around me, but couldn't make out any details. Then and there I began to ask Him if He'd help me see Him ever-more clearly and make me more present than I'd ever been. Suddenly, I was walking down a hallway, escorted by that same attendant toward a little room I knew belonged to Sai Baba. As soon as I walked in, I realized that nothing had changed; everything still looked fuzzy. I told myself, *"This isn't what I asked for."* As soon as I thought that, that's when it all became crystal clear and I could see Lord Baba sitting on His bed. So excited that I could then see Him, I started to ramble.

After carrying on for a while, I realized that I didn't give my Guru a proper greeting; I didn't acknowledge Him. So, I dropped to the floor to bow and show my respect. I knew this was not about Him getting praise, but about me learning the humility I needed to grow from apprentice to Master myself. As my forehead touched the floor, I looked up to see Baba also bowing to me. I was so blown away by *His* humility that that in itself humbled me to a level I'd never known before.

Through His gesture, Baba helped me to feel equal to Him. I was blessed to see what could happen when true respect and humility is practiced in God. I took the next few days to soak up and process the humbling experience that I had with Baba before I asked to see Him again.

After about four days, back at it I went. "Baba? If you are willing, I'd like another moment with you." That same night, Baba showed up again, but this time, He brought my deceased sister, Cheryl, which filled my heart with immense joy. After my consciousness stabilized, Baba began to speak.

"Keith, come over here and sit on the bed next to Cheryl and I." Baba was at the foot of the bed, while my sister and I sat at the headboard. When I looked at Sai Baba, He was tying His shoes. I thought to myself, *"Well that's weird. He never wears shoes."* Just then, Cheryl chimed in and said, "The true agenda of many governments and governmental figures worldwide will be brought to light. The United States – 'the greatest country of all' – with 'the greatest form of government' – will suffer a major breakdown. Its present legislative branch is going to collapse, and it will take years to rebuild it. Because of this restoration process, many old guard politicians will be forced out. Your new lawmakers will not make law, per se, but, rather, will introduce you to Divine Law and teach you how to fall into flow with It." Baba then said to both of us, "Wow! I can see I have two brilliant souls here with Me today." It was so great to see Cheryl again.

A week later, on my way to a gig, I wondered if some of my

flight attendant friends would be there to hear me play. My plan was to ask them if they had any leftover buddy passes they could share in case another one of my friends wanted to go India with me. Well, as Spirit would have it, when I walked through the gate at the club, I saw all three of them sitting there waiting.

These manifestations show how being in tuned with Spirit can be rewarding in the sense that one may not have seen such things if one were not tuned. The best part of that experience was, even though I wasn't sure if I was ever going to need the passes, all three were willing to give some to me.

The day was drawing nigh when I was to leave for India to see my Beloved Baba. Still needing to wrap up more things surrounding my trip, one day, I decided to go to the bank for traveler's checks. When I got there, the lady behind the desk asked me where I was going and why. After telling her about how my trip to see Baba and how the tickets came about, her face had completely changed from one of listening politely to an amazed, puzzled curiosity.

I'd say that she was a fundamental Christian, only because I've seen this sort of reaction by many of them whenever I would share such stories. This is not meant out of any sort of judgment. It's just that I live in the Bible Belt and know how most people of the Christian faith view these types of things. But I've never seen such curiosity in all my life.

After about fifteen minutes of speaking with the lady at the bank, I thanked her for helping me, shook her hand and walked out of her office.

After I got in my truck, it dawned on me why she so badly wanted to understand what I shared. I think she saw the sincerity in what I said, but what puzzled her was how I could be so jazzed up about any path other than Christianity. In hindsight, I wish I could've sat and shared with her how our paths are the same in their own beautiful way. How God is God – her God – my God – our God. And to also tell her not to be afraid for me, because I wasn't afraid for her.

The next day I went to Debbie's house (the lady who gave me the ticket for India) to find out my flight times. While I was there, she asked if I could go into a meditation and listen to guidance for her. I said, "Sure." How could I say no?

While in a meditative state, I saw Baba pull a lingam (a gold egg that represents the birth of Creation) out of His mouth and then hand it to me. When I came out of the meditation, I told her that the lingam was created out of Sai Baba's heart and that it was a gift to her for what she was doing for me. Baba told me to take this metaphorical lingam and pass it to her and tell her to swallow it. He also told me to tell her that many other gifts were coming her way. Debbie then asked if there was anything else. I told her the last part of the meditation was for me. She asked if I could tell her about it. I said, "Yes."

As I was coming out of the experience, Baba told me that my trip would be safe, blissful, upbeat and positive. Debbie and I chatted for about an hour longer, then I left to go back to my apartment.

As soon as I got home, I called my mother and father in South Louisiana to say hi and to let them know that I'd be leaving for India come Monday. Of course, Mom shared her deep concern about me going halfway around the world, but also told me to have fun, be safe and that she loved me greatly. After speaking to her for a while longer, my father took the phone.

Dad started off the conversation by sharing his love and then his concern. He told me of a program he saw on The Learning Channel that talked about false prophets, thinking that Baba was one of them. What he described did kind of sound like Baba, but the person that he had concerns with was wearing two pieces of clothing. I've never known Baba to wear anything but one-pieced gowns. Dad continued saying how the show exposed whoever this person was would fake manifestations. I told him not to worry and that he raised his son very well. I then told my parents goodbye, I loved them and I'd call on Monday before I boarded the plane.

I completely understood my parents' position. This path is not for everyone. But to speak on behalf of the "faker" in that program whoever it may be, provided that they are a true Master, and not a charlatan, there are reasons why a great teacher would do such a thing.

Why? To mirror to people their own beliefs about what they think is real or not. That is one reason why good magicians will never tell you their secrets. Because part of their "job" is to expand your imagination and get you to ponder the possibility that something magical can actually happen. But there's an absolute difference between a Master Teacher and a charlatan, and the judgment call should come from sincere inquiry into the life of the one in question. "What is the message of said person's life?" is the question I would ask.

The following evening, I went to see a movie with Kimmie. It was a wonderful night to be out and about, especially because of the lunar eclipse that was taking place. We went inside the theatre unsure about what to see, but eventually we settled on *Anna and the King*. Though I did enjoy the movie, what got me fired up were the many magical things that reminded me of Baba and His playful way. I will explain.

First, keep in mind that everyone on Baba's ashram always greets each other with "Sai Ram." It is an act of respect to greet someone by calling them one of God's many names.

Secondly, King Mongkut (Siam) would represent Sai Baba (Sai Ram). They both have royal families – Divine families. Those who follow Baba consider Him to be one of the many Kings (Saviors) that have come to the world. Likewise, King Mongkut was a good king with the same purpose to liberate people. The movie was filled with talk of enlightenment and learning a higher way of living.

Thirdly, at the end of the movie, I noticed a group of people from India which I saw as an amazing alignment with my trip that would soon take place. As you might imagine, I started feeling really jazzed about how we were led to this flick to see the interplay of Baba, knowing He was preparing me for the miracles that would happen when I got to the ashram.

As Kimmie and I were exiting the theatre, I looked up at the moon; it was in the total eclipse phase. It couldn't have been any more perfect until a huge flock of ducks, very high up, flew right underneath the celestial event. I started to freak out! The message I was getting from all the coincidences in the movie, the theatre, the eclipse and the flock of ducks was grace. I've read many books about different animals and what it means when they do certain things, and ducks flying represent grace.

Now, what could all of that possibly mean? Well let's start from the top.

Those who follow Sai Baba are considered His children, while the Siam family are *his* children. The group of people from India was referring to my soon-to-be destination.

Eclipses have always been a sign of great change. As for my life and what was about to happen over the next two weeks, that would definitely apply! I mean, how could it not, especially when you are going to be in the presence of the One you regard as God. Seeing the flock of ducks that night was Sai Baba telling me that, when you intentfully look into the darkness to find Me, My grace will become visible. And finally, the ducks under the eclipse told me that that grace in dark times will spark major change for me, but I had to look, "Up!"

After dropping Kimmie off at her house, I decided to go home to get some much-needed rest and start mentally preparing for my journey.

India Bound

I left home a just bit ago and I'm almost at the Memphis International Airport where I'll board a plane for India. My excitement and anticipation are high, as my want to be there overwhelms me. The first flight from Memphis to Detroit should be a piece of cake.

Now inside the airport, I'm walking around looking for where I'm supposed to check in.

Up to the desk I go to speak to a good-looking young man wearing a smile from ear to ear.

"Hello. Can I help you?" asks the gentleman.

"Yes," I say to him, as I hand my ticket over.

"How are you today, sir?" he says.

"You have no idea!" I reply.

"What does that mean?" he asks.

"Oh, nothing. I'm just excited about my trip."

"Yeah, I see you are going to India (*looking at my ticket*). What is in India that would have you travel there, and alone at that?" he continues.

"An Avatar," I say.

"Really?" he replies.

"Do you know what ..."

"... what an Avatar is? Yes, I do. I follow one there by the name of Sai Baba. Ever heard of Him?" he says.

"That's who ..."

"... you are going to see. I know," says the young man confidently.

"How in the world could you know that?" I ask puzzled.

"That I *don't* know," he replies, with an even bigger smile on his face than before. "Well, if you don't want to miss your plane, you better get going," he says, sending me off with silent well-wishes.

Here at Gate B11, I find a seat, sit down and wait to board the plane that will take me to my Baba.

"Attention passengers: We are now boarding for Flight 4705 from Memphis to Detroit," announces the lady behind the desk.

"Oh, my God, here we go!" I say to myself excitedly and somewhat scared to death.

After storing my luggage in the cubby, I sit down, strap in and ready myself for takeoff. Looking for something to distract me from my nervousness about flying, I reach for the bag of chips I bought in a shop at the airport.

"Hello passengers. This is your captain, Mark Rush. Welcome aboard Flight 4705 outbound from Memphis to Detroit. We have a smooth ride ahead of us and should arrive at our destination a few minutes ahead of schedule. Enjoy the flight and have a great day!"

Taxiing down the runway, the plane begins to pick up speed … faster … faster … faster … and here we go, up, up, up (*grabbing the seat for dear life*).

The plane has just leveled off at 41,000 feet and none too soon! Now, I can relax for the next hour.

"Would you like something to drink, sir?" says a pretty, brown-haired flight attendant, smiling as if I was the only one on the plane.

"Orange juice will do just fine," I reply.

"My name is Lisa. Let me know if there is anything I can do for you while you are on this flight."

"I will. Thank you!"

I've been flying for about 45 minutes now, and the captain just came on the PA system telling us that we were about to start our descent into Detroit.

With the plane landed and docked, I'm getting my bag out of the overhead storage and waiting to exit the craft. Then, I'll go the next gate to wait, wait and wait for the long haul overseas.

I just boarded the plane to Amsterdam. This flight is going

to be about seven hours or so which will give me some time to catch up on much-needed rest. I haven't been sleeping, you know. I've been thinking about this trip for three months and it's been a little tough to get a full eight hours due to all of the excitement.

As I make my way over the Atlantic Ocean to Holland, I thought I'd ask for something to eat and drink.

"May I help you, sir?"

"Yes. Do you have some vegetables or anything without meat?" I ask the flight attendant.

"Yes, we have fish and a vegetable medley that was left over from the dinner service."

"That'll do just fine."

I dive into the so-so tasting meal, grateful to have it. Upon finishing the last bite, I let out a big yawn thinking about that much-needed rest. I slouch down in my seat trying to get as comfortable as I can, let out another all-consuming yawn and drift off fast asleep.

"Good morning, passengers. We are starting our descent into Amsterdam Airport Schiphol. Have a fantastic day!" announced the good captain.

I open my eyes, sit up and look down the aisle of a dimly-lit plane to see the flight attendant coming my way.

"Am I seeing correctly?" wiping my eyes, hoping to clear any foggy vision from sleeping. I look again, only to see what looks like Sai Baba superimposed over the lady who tended to me ... and "They" are coming my way! My heart is racing faster than a thoroughbred coming out of the gate at the Kentucky Derby.

"This can't be happening!"

"You must begin to let go and transcend all of your doubt, Keith," is what I hear from within while the image of Lord Baba continues toward me. "Why is it so hard for you to believe that I am on this plane watching over you, making sure you feel safe and comfortable? You seem to have had no trouble getting to the point of believing that I invited you to come to India to see Me, and here you sit. So now, take your faith a step further, and trust that I am here warming you up for what you are about to experience when you get to My ashram," is what I hear as the apparition sits in the empty seat next to me and disappears.

I'm so befuddled right now as I try to make sense of what just happened. I know what I saw and I know what my heart felt, but my logical mind won't stop contradicting the experience. This sounds like a perfect time to exercise detachment from the world and move into the realm of Sai Baba's magic and power.

"If this is only the beginning of what I'll experience on this pilgrimage, then I'm in it all the way! 'Doubt – you are no longer allowed here, nor on the sacred road to my Teacher Who has no limits!'"

Touching down in the Amsterdam Airport, I'm on fire from experiencing one of the things I've only read about. With my bag in hand, I rush off the plane and make my way to the next gate to sit and wait, wait, wait.

"Attention, passengers. We are now boarding Flight 1602 for Mumbai," says the gentleman behind the desk in a Danish accent. I'm waiting until the last moment to board the very large plane, because I want to see how many people are going to cram into this Airbus.

(Counting to myself) "498 – 499 – 500 – 501– 502 – 503 people are boarding this plane." Most of them are Indian – "I'd better get moving!"

Finding my way to my seat I'm left to wonder, "How in the world is this big ole hunk of metal ever going to get off the ground?" The technology today is so amazing that I marvel at it.

We just left the runway and up, up, up we go to 41,000 feet. Man, I can never get used to this ear-popping thing. "I wish I had some gum."

"Sir, would you care for a piece of gum to help with your

ears?" asks the elderly Angel of Mercy sitting next to me clad in a pretty blue outfit.

"Thank you, kindly!" I tell her.

"Where are you going?" she asks in a soft voice.

"I'm going to South India to see a holy man," I say proudly.

"Are you, now? What pray tell drives a young man like you to travel halfway around the world pursuing such things?" she asks, knowing that the answer she's going to get would be a good one.

"Fire ... Passion ... Enlightenment!"

"Hello, ma'am. Hello, sir. Can I get you anything?" asks a lady attendant.

"I will have a screwdriver ... make that a double," says my new friend, giving me a wink.

"Nothing for me, thanks," thinking about another siesta.

"Well, young man. It looks like you have a heck of a hitch ahead of you. I can scoot over to the next seat and give you a little more room so that you can sprawl out and get some beauty rest, if you like," she says in a playful way.

"I think I'll take you up on your offer."

In two minutes, I'm out like a light.

I'm awoken by the captain, "Attention, passengers, we are about to start our descent into Mumbai. Please make sure your trays and seats are in their upright position as we prepare to land."

Leaving the plane, I notice a feeling present in my body. It's not hunger or the bathroom calling. I think it's actually knowing I'm now in India, closer to the Master I long to be with. "Stay focused, Keith." I hear over and over within. No sooner than I hear this message, I see an armed soldier standing by a desk looking at me. "Whoa!" I smile and say hello to a tall man who is there to serve and protect. As I walk around the airport searching for a place to squat for the next six hours, I see a bathroom and decide to head that way to freshen up.

"What in the God's creation is that ungodly smell? Mothballs!" I think, as I pinch my nose and enter the facility.

Finished with my business at hand, I walk out of the restroom and lay eyes on the sweetest, little piece of cement a guy seeking his Teacher could ever ask for. When I get there, I drop down like a sack of potatoes and go into meditation, knowing that this spot and I will become very acquainted for quite a while.

Just out of my meditation, I get up and walk around the airport to see what I can see. I notice more armed guards, very few people of the Caucasian persuasion and lots of Indians dressed in bright clothing. It seems to be a little tough to stay focused with all these new things around me. My mind really wants to engage in thought when what I should be doing is just take it all in without judgment.

"Hey, look! A vending stand."

"Hello, sir. How are you?" I ask a short-statured Indian man.

With very few words, all he could do to converse with me is point to the items he assumes I'd like. After going through the whole gamut, I settle on the bag of cookies and soda he pointed to first.

"Thank you!" I say, as I head back toward my little piece of real estate to eat my food and to wait, wait, wait.

Just as I sit down, the guard at the desk walks over.

"Sir? You stay right here and I will tell you when and where you have to go," he told me.

"How do you even know what that is?" I ask, thinking that he might be some sort of psychic.

"I've been watching people come through this airport for a very long time. All that come, I know where they are going and why. Though they all might look different to you, to me, they all look the same. And, I know that you are going to see Sai Baba," he says, while bobbling his head.

Yet, again, I'm completely befuddled by the events that are happening around me on my journey so far. I can feel an opening take place within, preparing me for something great while I'm on the ashram – I know it!

With a somewhat full belly, I use my backpack as a make-do pillow and go in for another time-killing slumber.

"Sir? Wake up!" says the armed guard, nudging me with the butt of his rifle.

"Yes?" I say freaking out, seeing his gun.

"Your plane is ready to take you to your Baba. (*Pointing*) Go down there and turn left and then take the second hallway to the right. You will find it. Don't worry, be happy!" he says, knowing that his contribution to my trip was helpful.

"Thank you very much!" I reply, as I grab my backpack and race to the final plane that will take me to my Master.

As I board, settle in the seat and leave Mumbai Airport, I can't think of anything else other than being with Baba.

At this point in my life, I'm beginning to understand the Love that happens between an aspirant and his Guru – true devotion on both parts. That's where the magic is. The devotion of the Teacher is the positive current and the devotion of the student is the negative current. It's this kind of synergy that makes peace, healing, expansion and self-realization in one's life possible.

Sitting aboard Flight 1740 at 37,000 feet, I'm headed to Bangalore, India. From there, I will seek out a taxi or a bus that will travel four hours over unpaved road to take me to my final destination – Puttaparthi – Prashanti Nilayam (The Abode of Highest Peace) – Baba!

"Hello, how are you today?" says a red-haired American man.

"I'm doing just great, thanks!" I reply, happy to see something familiar.

"Where are you going?" he asks.

"I'm going to see a holy man that came to me in a dream and told me to come to Him."

"Are you, now?"

"Where are you headed?"

"I am going to Bangalore to represent the company I work for in Seattle. I come here about twice a year for about a week at a time. If you don't mind, I am kind of tired and really need to get some rest. I hope you have fun on your journey to your holy man. Very nice to meet you," he tells me, reclining in his seat and going in for a nap.

Everything seems so surreal that I'm starting to feel love-drunk. *Well, it won't be long now. Just a few more hours and I will be with my Beloved Baba.*

Just as I finish a bag of those yummy airline peanuts and something to drink, a gorgeous Indian flight attendant walks over to me and says, "Sir? Would you like a message?" *"A message ... from Baba?" I think to myself.*

"A message, what kind of message?" I ask her.

"No. Would you like a massage?" she says in her best attempt. "I have an older sister in Bangalore who has a little shop there. You look like you been traveling a long time and could use some rest and relaxation."

"Oh! Thank you, but I have to be in Puttaparthi at a certain time."

"You are going to see Baba!" she tells me, somehow knowing what the armed guard in Mumbai knew. *"How do they do that?" I wonder.*

"Yes! Baba."

"We will be landing soon," she says with a wink, then leaves to secure the other passengers for our descent into South India.

On the ground and docked in Bangalore with no patience to exit, I'm doing all that I can to finally get out of this flying in a plane biz and into flying high.

As I walk into the airport and begin to look around for signs of catching a cab, people are immediately coming up to me and asking if I need a ride somewhere. *"Well, that was easier than I thought."*

"Follow me, sir!" they all say, bobbling their heads.

Something inside of me is telling me not to follow any of them. So, I'm going to go with my gut.

"I wonder what's over there?"

"Turn left now! Walk down the hall … you see that lady … ask her where to go," I hear clearly within.

"Excuse me," I say, wondering if she understands.

"Yes. How can I help you, sir? Never mind. I know where you are going. You see that man over there?" she says pointing. "Go to him and ask him to take you to Baba."

"How do they do it – that knowing thing?" scratching my head.

"May I help you, sir?" asks the gentleman, stomping on a cigarette. "Baba?" he says, knowing like they all do.

"Yes! Baba," I reply, amazed at what appears to be guidance wherever I go.

"Follow me. I will take you to a taxi nearby," says the nice man, bobbing his head. *"Why do they do that bobble thing? What's that all about?"*

I climb into a little white cab with a young man who's going to drive me to Sai Baba's ashram.

After about fifteen minutes into the ride, the driver in his thick Indian accent tells me, "It is about a four-hour ride so sit back and relax."

"I know how to do that," I reply, as I fall further into the seat and take in the view of the countryside.

Finally, on the dirt road that'll take me to my Baba, I think about how my journey is unfolding and to make sure that I keep logging everything for a future book – this book.

All my flights from Memphis until today came off without a hitch. In fact, I had an apparition of Baba on the plane from the US to Amsterdam, as well as some nice synchronicity with helpful people along the way. Although the flights were grueling and the layovers were long, believe me when I tell you that you have to really want to go to India to ever gain what it has to offer.

I'm looking down at the clutter of notes I have about my trip so far … when out of nowhere … I hear, "Honk! Honk! Beep! Beep!" as the cab begins to swerve on the road. I look up and grab the seat with a grip so tight, you can bet my fingers left imprints.

"What is it?" I ask startled.

"Oh, my friend, don't worry. Be happy! I have everything under control. This is how we drive here," he says to me in his best attempt at English.

"I think I'll do that!" pocketing my notes and hoping his advice will alleviate my anxiety.

"What's your name?" I ask.

"My name is Basa."

"I'm Keith."

"It is nice to meet you, Mr. Keith."

Feeling a little more relaxed, I look around and notice not only the cute, hut-like houses and village, but also, how crazy people drive here. Everyone seems to be everywhere on the road with no designated lanes for anything. But somehow, at the right time, everyone knows exactly what the others are going to do, and so, they do the opposite. Strangely, they have order in what I see as chaos.

"Taxies in India have the right of way. Everyone else will move for us," he says with a laugh, knowing what I just went through.

"I'm definitely cool with that, my friend!" finally releasing my grip from the seat.

As endless vehicles whiz by, I notice that all the trucks are donned with festive colors, like Mardi Gras from my birthplace in South Louisiana. So many rickshaws, so many people, so many monkeys – "Monkeys! …. What?" I see oxen with their horns painted blue and yellow and believe it or not – elephants. What a trip!

"What in the world is that? No way! Is that a motorbike that

just flew past with an entire family atop it?" As I look closer, I see what seems to be the father driving, a little girl on his lap, two children sandwiched between the father and the mother who's on back, and behind the mother is yet another little kid holding on for dear life.

"Now what's that?" There are not two, but three men on a motorbike. Talk about a culture shock!

As I look all around, I can see children playing and making fun out of the simplest of things to be found. It kind of reminds me of my youth and how creative we all are in our innocence. Sweet!

I'm about an hour into the ride and I'm starting to make some sense of, or at least accepting, their way of life. One thing I can't seem to accept so readily is all the poverty. But who am I to say what is poor? I know they live simple lives and that's probably all they've ever known. For all I know, they may be rich and full within themselves. I'd think that they are since they do not have the distractions like we have in the West and are probably able to focus more on that which is real.

In the little villages and townships, these people don't earn a living. They make a living. They get up early every day, till the land, plant seeds, nurture them and harvest their food, all the while doing chores that are congruent with their day-to-day survival. It seems they take great pride in all that they do and are grateful for the work that needs to be done. Not like Westerners who'll just pick up the phone and hire outside help to try to make our life a little freer. We seek recreational time to find fulfillment from that which we partake in. *"Ah, yes!"* As I look around again, it definitely seems they have a much richer sense of Self here.

When I got off the plane in Bangalore, I didn't see this self-made ideal so much. It was more a tone of, "Hey ... a tourist! Let's talk him out of his money with an offer to do something in return." I'd bet that these particular people have televisions and are chasing more of the American model. I can see why.

I have to admit that we in the West are fortunate to not only earn a living, but to have the time and freedom to live alternate lives. We go out to socialize in bars and clubs, we go to parks and we play sports of all different kinds. We are able to do so much in cities all across America.

I'm quite aware that we have our own poor communities as well, but they are still Americanized to some degree. I think the day will come when the East and West will share what each has to offer. I also think that this would be true the world over. This has to be part of the Divine Plan. I understand that diversity is beautiful, but definitely not at the expense of one having more than the other. Diversity and equality have to be the two sides of the spiritual coin.

I'm humbled by what I see – the people, how they live and what the Earth and God mean to them. All in all, I'm starting to fall in love with India.

Leaning back in my seat and letting out a big yawn, I'm beginning to feel the toll of many hours in transit. Although I can feel the tiredness deep in my bones, I realize that it's just a matter of a few hours until I get to Sai Baba's ashram.

All of a sudden – "BANG!" – an energy – a force, a burst of Light happens from within, giving me what I need to go forth with a wakeful mind, a ready heart and happy feet.

Right now, I'm having all kinds of preconceived notions running through my head about what awaits me. Though this was to be expected, I did promise myself before I left Memphis that I'd not get lost in my ideas and ask God to help me find His in me. Still and all, it's a challenge and a purposeful one, helping me to see how busy minded I can be in my daily life. But I've decided not here and not now. I came all this way to see and be with God, and dang it, that is exactly what I'm going to do!

In my conviction, I take my shoes off and relax further into the ride. Feeling the warmth on my face from the open taxicab windows, I can't help but notice how beautiful is the day. Clear, sunny, the temperature is perfect; the sky is as blue as it can possibly be – just a gorgeous day to be on such a journey.

It's still somewhat tough to get used to the way people drive here. They will not hesitate for a moment to use the wrong lane to push anyone out of the way who doesn't have priority cargo. Everyone knows who has the right of way. It seems to be some sort of non-spoken agreement. And, I can tell you it's such a hoot to watch.

What an amazing change of pace it is for me to see all this diversity; like the three men that passed by on one motorcycle. Back in the States, some would deem these people as gay or weird, but that's just not the way it is here. They see something like this simply as a way of transport from one place to another, and I'm amazed at the change in consciousness from America to here in India.

As we turn down another little country road, I can see lots of trees with pretty orange and yellow flowers. The landscape reminds me of something I read in a book about Baba. In it, Baba states, "Your trip here, especially if you are coming from the States, will wear you down in all aspects. It is very good that you arrive this way. This preparation is to make you open and ready to receive all the reasons you are here." If that's true, then I'm going to be receiving a lot because I'm beat!

Now, I can see why Sai Baba's thought came to me. When we turned down this road, what went through my head was how tired I actually am.

"What's that noise?" asks the driver.

I'm wondering, *"What's wrong?"* as the driver pulls the car over, gets out, opens the hood and begins to fidget with some things. After a couple of minutes, he shuts the hood, walks over to the front passenger side of the car and gives the tire a couple of good kicks. Then he wipes his hands on what seems to be a mechanically-soiled handkerchief, comes back to the car, opens the door, sits down, and starts the engine along with a few heavy-footed accelerations.

"Is everything alright?" I ask him.

He turns and looks over his shoulder and says, "Don't worry, be happy!"

"I'm happy as a lark," I say, as he drives towards the ashram.

Since the conversation has started up again with my new friend, I decide to take a little break from writing in my journal to chat for a bit.

"Basa. How often do you drive to Baba's ashram?"

"On a slow day, I will make the journey twice to drop off visitors there. On a long day, I will make the trip three times," he says, bobbing his head all around.

"Why do they do that bobbing head thing?" I wonder if it's when the life-force energy moves through their bodies and gets filtered by their consciousness that it creates this back and forth circular motion?

"The band I play with back in Memphis just started a gig at 9pm their time, and it's 9am here. That would be a twelve-hour difference between us." Thinking about time and space, I go into some deep thinking about the Infinity of God and how it is all relative.

"Beep! Beep!" "Toot! Toot!" "Augha!" The car horns continue to sound off as it appears … we are going to collide with the others coming this way. *"No … I just can't seem to get used to this!"* Even so, what's weird about this experience with the drivers is that it seems to have opened a door for me so I can see myself and where I am in my feeling base. Along with any remaining anxiety from the lack of road rules here is an apprehension about what lies ahead of me on this sojourn. In contrast, I'm pretty darned excited!

Looking back, I suspected this kind of intuition and energy play would happen when I came on this trip; lots of bipolar swinging; Sai Baba as Divine Father would push me as hard as He knew I needed, and as Divine Mother, would be nurturing, kind and supportive. It's my guess that Baba is doing this so I can a find balance in the dance. And, on top of all that energetic movement, you can add a large dose of being out of place.

Think about it. I'm a young man all by myself in India, not knowing a soul or where I am, nor what lies ahead of me. But it seems that my fear about anything is beginning to subside and I'm starting to relax into the situation. I must be feeling Baba.

"Yes … that's it! It's the soft trust that will sustain me in times of uncertainty. I get it!" That's the exact kind of stuff I'm here to experience; those magical, miraculous glimpses of Spirit and the flubs of being human. In this way, I can refine my choices to create a fantastic life.

I must acknowledge the longing I have deep within me; this feeling for me right here and right now doesn't seem to be an illusion as with my fear about things. I don't think this longing has a negative charge from a missing home and friends kind of thing. It's more a yearning; like there's an incredible hole inside; like being hungry for food, but that doesn't quite describe it either. Whatever it is, I sure hope that in this void lies enough manna to sustain me on my trip and for the rest of my life.

"Mr. Keith. Do you want something to drink?" asks Basa.

"No, thank you. I will pass for now."

"Why is it so hard for me to let go and participate fully in my own journey. What's up with that?" Boy, I sure have work to do while I'm here, that's for certain.

"I take that back. Yes. I'd love something to drink."

"I have noticed that since we left the airport you have been speaking into your recorder and writing a lot. What is that for?" Basa asks.

"For a future book about my time here in India and with Baba."

"Oh, so you are an author."

"Well, I guess you can say I'm working on that."

"Do you have another ink pen?"

"Yes. I have a few of them. Why do you ask?"

"Because we are about to pull into a little town a mile down the road and there will be young children who would love to have one," he says.

"How many children will there be?" I ask him.

"About seven or eight."

"Just one ink pen for that many kids?" I ask not understanding.

"Oh, Mr. Keith, trust me! They will know what to do with it."

"Sure. I'll give it to them."

"Okay, we are here," says Basa, as he stops the car, gets out and begins to call to the children playing on and around a rope swing.

"Mr. Keith, you play with the children while I go inside and get our drinks."

I step out of the car only to see a group of excited kids running to me as fast they possibly can.

"Mister! Mister!" say eight bright-eyed children, bouncing up and down as they surround me.

"Do you have something for us?" asks a precious little girl in her best attempt at English.

"As a matter of fact, I do, young lady!"

"Please! Please! Can we have it?" they all sound off in unison.

"Yes!" I tell them, still unsure about how I will divide the ink pen between them.

"Keith, draw watches and rings on their arms and fingers with your ink pen," I hear clearly within.

"Come here, little girl," I say, as I reveal the gift.

"Can I have it?" she asks.

"Not just yet. Give me your arm," I say to her, as I bend over and begin to draw a watch and a ring on her finger.

Excited about her new jewelry, the little girl runs inside a nearby house shouting, "Amma!" and shows it to her mother.

"Do me next ... Do me next!" say the remaining children, all with the arms high up in the air.

"Mr. Keith, I have us two soda pops. Leave the pen with the last child. We must be going now," Basa tells me.

"Goodbye and have fun!" I tell the children who just stole my heart.

Once we are on the road again, Basa says, "Some of the people in this little village will only eat once a month."

Oh, how my heart hurts whenever I hear such a thing. I'm sure there will be plenty of chances for me to deepen my compassion while in India. And, to be perfectly honest, I feel that compassion is one of the main reasons I'm here. It's a feeling that I love having, but it usually arises in me when there's a reason for it. I just wish that feeling would be with me all of the time because, when I'm in a compassionate state, that's when I actually feel the Love of God.

After riding on the road for about another hour, Basa asks me the most profound question I ever had put to me in my life.

"Sir? Are you ready to meet Sai Baba?"

"You have no idea!" I say excitedly.

"Good. Because we are here!"

Lessons In Love

I can't begin to describe what I'm feeling in this moment. What's the feeling a person is supposed to have when they are at the golden gate of God's domain, knowing He's there waiting for them: nervousness – fear? Well, what I feel is elation and lots of it!

The taxi just passed through Baba's ashram gates and I can't sit still as you might imagine. Everything seems so swirly, so surreal. I can only describe it as I did before; it's like being drunk on love in a dream.

The car comes to a stop at the orientation office where I get out, shut the door, pay Basa, and thank him for his company and the exhilarating ride. As he drives away, I look all around and take in a full view of this beautiful place where so many people come to witness the Divinity that lives in this abode. Right now, I feel safer than I have since I've started my trip. Taking in a deep breath and exhaling with a sigh, I walk to the office to sign in.

Approaching the desk, a man behind it asks me, "Sai Ram (*acknowledging God within another*), did you come here alone or with someone else?"

"I'm here by myself," I reply.

"Then I will partner you up with someone," he says. "Have you ever seen Baba before?" he asks, already knowing the answer.

"No," I reply in an antsy tone.

"Sai Ram, leave your bags here, they are safe. Go down this street, just pass the bookstore to the right; you will see the Kulwant Hall where Baba will be coming out shortly for this afternoon's darshan (*blessings from a holy man*)."

"There's the bookstore ... there's that slight, right turn ... and there's Kulwant Hall." With my heart pounding from the run and from what is about to happen, I arrive at the hall.

Walking into the entrance, I'm greeted by someone, "Sai Ram, you must take your shoes off to enter."

"Thank you!" I reply.

As I walk through a metal detector, I take the time to slow down my panting from running and to show respect. There are many people here – thousands! I guess the only place for me to sit is in the back; probably a good idea so that I can see just how things are done. In addition, I promised myself that I wouldn't do any "work" today, just observe.

Sitting on the back row, I look up, down and all around, as my mind begins to ramble, *"Oh, wow! The ceilings are made of gold. Of course, they are! Why wouldn't they be? Men on one side and ladies on the other. Yep. Just like I'd read about."*

The reason the men and women are separated is to eliminate any distractions, making it easier to focus on one's development and not on the object of one's lust.

There's some Indian music playing throughout the hall, along with multiple thousands of people murmuring on top of that. I'm beginning to feel an overwhelming humility – a feeling of insignificance in comparison to the Grand Scheme. I guess this is the disposition Lord Baba talks about that I'm supposed to have, making me available for what is Present.

All of a sudden, the music and the thousands of people become silent and everyone is looking to the little gate on the right. *"What's going on? Oh, my God ... Sai Baba must be coming!"*

Out of thin air it seems, a little figure walks through the gate on the women's side. *(Pinching myself)* *"Is this for real? I'm here in India and that is Bhagwan Sathya Sai Baba!"* His entrance is a Greatness like I've never imagined one could possibly possess. He has a Presence and Light so expanded that it's engulfing everyone and everything near Him. I can actually see it! Now, I understand the humility and the feeling I had when I first got into Kulwant Hall.

Baba is now walking around the women's side, taking letters

and manifesting things. *"How awesome!"*

Slowly, but surely, Baba is making His way to the men's side of the hall doing the same thing, and during this whole time, He's blessing all with hand gestures, always giving whoever He talks to His full, undivided attention. I can see how He is the Love He has for people. He's also pointing to a few here and a few there, granting them a one-on-one interview when darshan is over. I sure wish I could be so lucky.

"Oh, no! I've got it now, too. The dreaded ashram disease – interviewitis." I was told about that. That same someone also told me, "What you should want more than an interview is an inner view." I agreed, but who wouldn't still want to meet the Cosmic Christ?

Before you know it, Sai Baba goes into the room with those He selected to grant them their interviews and the darshan is over.

I guess the best thing for me to do now is to go back to the orientation office, collect my bags and get settled in my room and meet my roommate.

Leaving Kulwant Hall I feel much lighter, and I'm so ready for these two weeks of lessons in Love.

That Feeling!

Wondering what my room is going to be like, I open the door to find a basic hotel layout: two cot-style beds, two recessed closets for hanging up clothes, and a bathroom with a toilet and shower. As I look around appreciating the clean, little room and nodding my head, the door opens with a loud squeak, "Hi! I'm Damiere ... we have the same birthday!" he says, in a deep, guttural Croatian accent.

"We do? Well, ain't that special! I'm Keith Blanchard," I say, shaking his hand.

"Damiere, where'd you get those cool clothes?"

"They are called Punjabis, and you can buy them at the store here on the ashram."

"Would you please show me a little later where that store is?"

"Sure. What are you doing right now?" he asks, with an offer in his voice.

"Maybe do some bhajans (*singing songs to God*) in the Kulwant Hall."

"Okay then. I'll see you when I see you," my new friend says, chuckling.

Leaving the room, I feel somewhat awkward because I didn't ask Damiere if he wanted to come with me to explore the ashram. It's just that it seems he wants to become arm-in-arm buds, when all I want to do right now is go out on my own and take it all in.

I just got back to the room from my long stroll around this beautiful ashram and the trip I took with Damiere to get some of that cool ashram wear. I think I'm going to retire for the night.

"Boy, am I tired," letting out a big yawn.

"Yes, me, too," says Damiere.

"Good night, my Brother."

"Good night, Keith."

It's about 4:15 in the morning when I'm awakened by the many sounds coming from outside my room: shuffling feet, coughs, grunts and mumbles from all the people making their way down to Kulwant Hall to experience Sathya Sai Baba.

Yes, I know I'm a little slow to rise, but I'm not yet mentally prepared from all that traveling, and besides, I need to attend to my rumbling belly. I think I'll grab a snack from my bag and eat it in the courtyard before I start my big day.

Sitting on a bench and nibbling on some cheese crackers, I don't know what to think about all this. This is my first real day in a two-week crash course in God, and while my heart is wide open and ready to receive the Master, my mind is presenting resistance.

The courtyard is empty as I'm sure everyone is on their way to Kulwant Hall. Looking at the morning sky, I take the last bite of my food and drink some bottled water. You wouldn't believe how many packs of these little snacks I brought with me. I have a PC laptop carrying case full of them. Well, I had to be prepared.

It's about 4:30am (*looking at my watch*). "*I'd better get down to the hall.*"

Walking down the path towards Lord Baba, I hear crickets, frogs and birds announcing the new day in a symphony of sounds. It's just so amazing here on the ashram in all its peacefulness.

Upon arriving right outside Kulwant Hall, I can see everyone is taking their shoes off. "*I guess I'd better do the same.*"

Following the other men, I come to a place where I see everyone sitting and waiting in one of about sixteen lines. Even though I'm late getting down here, I feel very fortunate to get a spot in line 3. "*Yeah, this spot will do just fine. This has to put me in a real good position to see Baba.*"

"Sai Ram? I know what you are probably thinking," says an Indian man who turned around to talk to me.

"You do?"

"Yes!" he said.

"And, what's that?"

"You are thinking that just because you are sitting in this line you will be ushered in before most, and therefore, have a better seat for Baba. Am I right?"

"How can you possibly know that?" I ask. *Thinking that this man might have psychic powers, too.*

"Well, it's common knowledge, and besides, I have been here a few times before and know what a newbie looks and thinks like," he says, letting out a laugh.

"You're a funny man!" I exclaim.

"The way it works is, they call out the lines randomly and march you in that way. You must understand that it's Lord Baba who orchestrates who is going to sit where. Also, know that, when you come here, if you don't choose a place to sit right away, one of the Seva Dals (*someone of selfless service*) will do it for you, and you must comply."

"Thank you for the information, Sai Ram."

"You are welcome, my friend. Om Sai Ram," he says, as he turns back around.

Now that we're all sitting down, I'm thinking that they're likely going to be calling out the lines for us to go into the hall soon. (*Time goes by*) No such thing! It's been about an hour and a half, and we are still sitting here.

"Sai Ram, why do we have to get up so early if we don't see Baba till 7:15am?" I ask the gentleman in front of me.

"To teach us patience," he says, as we both start to laugh from my lesson learned.

"Line 5, stand up and make your way into the hall. Line 11, please stand up and make your way into the hall. Line 8, please stand and make your way into the hall," says a man holding a tablet. (*Crossing my fingers on both hands*) ... "Line 3 ... stand up and make your way into the hall." "Yes ... *that's my line! I guess I'd better get up and follow these men into the hall.*"

Just like yesterday, there's a Seva Dal guiding me through a metal detector. "Baba will be out soon," he says, winking at me, knowing this is my first trip to see Him. Again, how do they know these things?

As I pass through the metal detector, like everyone else, I race to search for what I think is the best place to sit.

On the second row I take my position, right here so as to be close to my Master when He gives us darshan (*blessing from a holy man*). I feel like a kid in a candy store.

People are steadily coming in the hall, and room to move around is becoming no room at all.

"What on Earth is that?" Off in the distance I hear music and it sounds like it's getting louder. *"What's going on? Sounds like a parade and it's getting closer. I see. It is a parade!"*

"Now what's that?" hearing something that sounds like chanting. "Where's that chanting coming from?" I ask the gentleman sitting next to me.

"Sai Ram, that is Suprabhatam," says a big man with very few teeth.

"What's that?" I ask with a burning curiosity.

"Ask Baba. If He wants you to know, He will lead you there," he says, as if knowing it would happen.

I can't seem to find where the chanting is coming from, but it sure is powerful! *"Oh, well. I guess I'll know about it when I'm supposed to know."*

"Bang! – Bang! – Bang!" I open my eyes and take notice of a huge, golden bell being rung, as everyone starts chanting, "Aum." (*Counting*) *"Eighteen ... nineteen ... twenty ... twenty-one. I wonder what the significance of the twenty-one chants is, and how come I didn't notice that bell yesterday?"*

"Sai Ram, please excuse me. What's the reason for the parade, the bell and the twenty-one 'Aum' mantra we just did?" I ask the American next to me.

"The parade celebrates God's on Earth, while the ceremonial bell simultaneously rings with the bells in the Court of the

Highest Order, awakening the Lord upon the Earth. The mantra represents our asking God to bless, protect, guide and tend to us this day," he warmheartedly shared.

So beautiful! Everything here is a ritual and celebration to that which matters most. It's such an amazing feeling to be around these many enlightened souls. At any moment, they're all willing to help your heart stay open for long periods of time.

It seems that yesterday I got here to the Kulwant Hall just after the bell rang and the mantra was over. But I can tell you that after chanting the twenty-one "Aums" just a bit ago with all these people, I feel more grounded and ready to see Sai Baba, not like this morning in the courtyard.

My attention is now back on what's taking place all around me, and I'm noticing that same Indian music playing that I heard yesterday. *"I'm guessing that Baba will be coming soon," I think to myself, as I close my eyes and go into prayer.*

The Hindi music just stopped. *"That must mean ... Baba!"* In all His Glory, through the gate walks God. If you would, stop reading for a bit and take that idea in. Just imagine if you were able to see God, in whatever deity of your choice. How would that be for you? Now, you know what I'm feeling. And that's very important to be able to "get" the true message of this book – that feeling!

With Baba in sight, I'm determined to watch every move He makes very closely. Not to try to catch Him in a slight of hands trick pretending to manifest something which I've read about before. But to get to know Him and what He might have for me through my diligent paying attention. Also, because I've read in many books that if you don't take your eyes off of Him for even just one second, He may grant you an interview. And so, yes, I have to admit that I still have some of that interviewitis bug that's going around.

Just like yesterday, Baba walks into the hall on the women's side giving them His darshan. He does this by waving, taking letters, manifesting things, pointing to some granting them an interview, and of course, blessing them with His gestures, gaze, touch and kind words.

As Baba makes His way over to the men's side of the hall, He is doing all the same things He did for the women.

"Oh, wow!" Sai Baba is right in front of me spinning His hand around in circles about to create something. Out of Baba's hand pours more ash than His hand can actually hold. The man Baba is doing this for is on his knees bowing, showing reverence for the grace. After blessing him, Baba turns down the last aisle and makes His way into the little room where He gives interviews. The darshan is over and I and many others are leaving Kulwant Hall. All in all, it lasted about 40 to 45 minutes.

Witnessing this was a big deal for me. It helped me to anchor what I already know: that manifesting at will is a very real phenomena, and natural in that there are Avatars (Divine Descents) here today who can actually do this.

Today, whenever Baba would manifest something, you could feel an amazing power move throughout the hall: from the creation of the object, to all the onlookers' focused attention on Baba doing it. There are no words I know to describe the feeling that is present when this little man turns His hand and out pops an object for all to see. I know that's not a satisfactory answer. So, I will do my best to describe what the experience feels like.

It's like we all create the objects together. I'm starting to wonder that since energy follows attention, does Sai Baba draw from everyone's excitement and use His and the people's one-pointed focus to assist in the manifesting? It's almost as if everyone shifts to the dimension from where such things come and we bring them back together. I hope my idea translates to you. Maybe some insight surrounding this will happen as my journey and this book unfold.

The fact that Sai Baba can materialize things spontaneously is evidence to me that He *is* an Avatar. What's even more impressive is the endless outpouring of Selfless Love that He bestows upon everyone here. To me, this is the real evidence of who He truly Is. I mean, He does darshan twice a day, every day, and every once in a while, other things, such as discourses or festivals to honor a particular day. But He doesn't really ever go anywhere nor do anything unless it's for those who come to see and be with Him.

I read once that Sai Baba went to South Africa to heal one of His devotees He knew was sick. You may ask, "Why didn't He just heal the man remotely?" My guess is that, it probably wouldn't have been enough. Can you imagine the man's level of devotion for Sai Baba to leave India and go all the way to South Africa? The man had to be so devoted that Baba knew he was not well and that the man's healing would come from the same devotion by showing up at his house. The reciprocal current is probably what healed the man. Like with the woman who touched Jesus' garment wanting to be healed, "It is your faith in Me that heals you."

Can you imagine the look upon the man's face, as well as how his heart felt, when he opened the door only to see Sai Baba standing there? That shift is what had to be the healing factor. This is a favorite story of mine and one of the best that portrays Baba as the Love He Is.

Though I've only been here for a day and a half, I'm starting to feel less empty than I did before. My guess is, by the time I get home, I'll likely be bloated with enough input that it'll take years to digest and assimilate.

Today was my second experience singing bhajans in the hall. It's spiritually uplifting to be among the thousands who sing songs to God. There are people from all over the world here: England, Iceland, Germany, France, Italy, China, Japan, Sweden, Africa, Russia, New Zealand, Turkey, South America, Australia, Thailand, Singapore – from every denomination: Hinduism, Christianity, Jainism, Judaism, Islam, Buddhism, Sikhism – and in every kind of profession: Monks, Clerks, Priests, Scientists, Doctors, Lawyers, Firemen, Policemen, Truck Drivers, Government Officials, Dentists, Waiters, Musicians – all here to see the Master that called them. And so, there is a natural flow with all who are "under the influence."

Like I said, everyone on the ashram calls everyone else "Sai Ram" (*I acknowledge God within you*). But, it doesn't only mean hello. It has a myriad of meanings like kindness, appreciation, politeness, thank you, my apology, excuse me, goodbye and many others. It's all the play of the Master who summoned us.

Leaving Kulwant Hall, I think I'll take in some more sites from around the ashram, as well as in the town, even though it's highly recommended that you stay put on the ashram grounds. I'm guessing the reason one should not venture out is because the focus should be on your growth and your growth alone. It's probably not beneficial to mix and mingle with all the chaos happening on the outside. But I'm going to do it anyway to buy some souvenir gifts for friends, and hopefully my Baba will guide me.

Standing at the ashram gates, I'm about to step into the street where there will be beggars of many kinds. I was told that if I did go out, I'd be approached by those who have maimed themselves for pity, some who actually rent babies claiming they need milk for the child, to some who have no compunction whatsoever about walking up to you and asking you for money.

I understand all of that and I'm okay with it. I just want to get a few things for my friends and myself to go into the shrine I'll create in my apartment for my Love of God. *"Here I go!"*

"Whoa!" There are people moving all over the place; up, down and sideways in the streets. All I can see are little tourist-like shops and everything in them are about Baba. *"Oh, no!"* Someone has locked eyes with me and is coming my way.

"Sai Ram ... help me, please! I need money to buy milk for the bay-bay. She is very hungry and needs it to make her feel better.

Help me, please!" she says desperately.

"I wish I could help you. Unfortunately, I can't at this time," I tell her, hoping that what appears to be a dire situation is all an act.

"But, you must! You must help the bay-bay. It is not for me. Please!" she says, coming across more convincing in her plight.

Even after learning that I'd be approached by beggars and that they are very good at it, I feel myself wanting to reach into my pocket.

"Sai Ram, look! My hands are not able to work to provide for my child. Please, for the Love of God, I ask you!" she continues on, knowing that I'm contemplating giving her some money.

"Here. I'll give you 53 rupees (*1 US dollar*)," I say to her, as I reach for my wallet.

"Thank you, but that is not enough! I need 106 rupees. Please!" she says, as if praying to me.

"I tell you what I'll do. I'll give you 269 rupees (*5 US dollars*). Will that be enough to buy your baby some milk?" I say, thinking that I'll have done my good deed for the day, as well as get me out of the awkward situation.

"Yes! Oh, thank you ... thank you!" she says, going down on her knees and kissing my hands.

"You're welcome," I tell her, trying to walk away, all the while blessing her in my mind and with my heart.

"Wow! Look at that cool Baba poster over there." I walk into the store and up to the counter.

"Sai Ram. Can I help you?" says the man behind the register.

"Yes, please. How much is that poster of Baba?" I ask, thinking how cool that five-foot photo would look over my fireplace.

"5,381 rupees," he says, trying to convince me that I'm getting a good bargain. *"Let's see ..."* *converting rupees into dollars in my mind.*

"One hundred dollars?" I say in disbelief.

"Yes, only for you today and right now!" he says, knowing

that I know he will not come down off of the price.

After tossing around the idea whether I should or shouldn't purchase that poster, my answer is the one that you think it is.

"Okay … I will take it," pulling the money out of my wallet to pay him.

The man takes down the poster, rolls it up, shoves it into a canister and hands it to me saying, "Thank you, Sai Ram." Proud as a peacock with my poster, I exit the store.

Looking around, I notice a young man standing on the corner where two streets intersect. Somehow, I feel that I should walk over there and talk with him.

"Hello, Sai Ram. How are you doing today?" I ask the good-looking youngster.

"Great! How are you?"

"Same as you. I'm Keith," reaching to shake his hand.

"I am named Sadru. What can I do for you, Mr. Keith?" he asks, in his Hindi laid-back way.

"Do you know where I can find the best shop around to buy some cool stuff that won't cost too much?" I ask him, somehow knowing that he will help me get the type of things I want.

"This way," he says, pointing down an alley and walking in that direction. "My father has a shop and is a good and honest man. He will take very good care of you," he tells me, with appreciation for the opportunity to make a day's wage.

"Father, meet Mr. – ? Remind me of your name, please."

"Keith … Keith Blanchard," I say, as I shake what appears to be a good man's hand, indeed.

"Hi, Mr. Keith! My name is Amish. What can I do for you?" he asks, in his soft and nonabrasive way.

"Now, I see where Sadru gets his character from."

Looking around at all the cool things in his shop, I ask, "How much do you want for the entire place?" (*laughing*)

"Oh, my friend, the shop will go to Sadru when I die and is not for sale," patting his son on the shoulder. "But you can have everything in it!" he says, as we all go into a chuckle. "Okay, so what would you like?" he asks me in a more serious tone.

"I'm serious. I want all of it or at least, close to it!" thinking how cool this stuff is going to look in my shrine.

"You just tell Sadru what you want and he will get them and have them ready for you. Do not hesitate to let me know if I can help you further," says Amish, as he heads toward a little room in the back.

"What do you want me to get for you first?" asks Sadru.

(*Pointing*) "I'll take three of those ... that over there ... give me five of those right there ... oh, yes ... I have to have that, too! (*Continuing on*) Definitely the big thing over there ... that gold Buddha figurine ... that statue of Baba, that jade japamala (*prayer bead*), etc.," I tell him, as his eyes begin to pop out of his head.

Trying to keep up with me, Sadru begins to pack up my items. After I hand him 1,400 US dollars, he tells me, "Wait here – I will be right back!" as he walks toward the same little room where his dad had gone.

"Mr. Keith! Please ... please, come this way," says Sadru, peeking out from a curtain with a smile on his face.

"Sit here, please!" pointing to his chair as a gesture of respect and appreciation.

"No, it's okay. I'll sit here instead."

"I will not have it any other way, Mr. Keith! Please, sit here in my chair."

"Okay. Thank you!"

"Sadru, get Mr. Keith anything he wants!"

"Yes, Baba (*Father*)!"

"I will be right back," says Amish.

Sadru and I've been chatting for about ten minutes when his dad comes back in, walks up to me with a cup in his hand and hands it to me.

"What's this?" I ask gratefully.

"This is Father's special Chai tea. He does not make this for just anyone, and you should consider this an honor!" says Sadru.

"Well then, I'd love some, Mr. Amish," knowing that what I'm about to experience from this cup is going to be ambrosia.

"No mister. Just plain ole Amish."

"Oh, my goodness!" I exclaim, tasting the tea.

"What is it? You do not like it?" he asks worriedly.

"It's amazing!" I say with a huge smile, sealing our eternal respect and friendship.

"May Lord Baba bless you; for you have brought much joy to me and my family!" says the teary-eyed man.

"Lord Baba *has* blessed me as to why I'm here drinking this wonderful tea and talking with you and Sadru."

"Raahi ... Raahi ... where are you?" shouts Amish, while looking into another room.

"Come here and take Mr. Keith's things wherever he wants. He has brought good fortune to our family. Make sure you don't break any of it or lose anything when in transport."

"Yes, Uncle. Right away!" says the young man.

"Sai Ram? Tell me. What are you going to do with all of these things?" asks Amish.

"Some of them are for me, others are for friends and family, but most of it is for a shrine to Lord Baba that I'll create in my home when I return."

"I understand. But do you have to take all of India back with you?" letting out a big laugh.

"It was nice to meet you, Mr. Keith," say Amish and Sadru.

"No mister. Just plain ole Keith," shaking their hands, then I walk out of the shop.

"Where are we going, Mr. Keith?" ask Raahi.

"We are going to my room on Baba's ashram."

"I will follow you," he says, as if at my beckoning call.

Now back at the room and somewhat overwhelmed by my venture outside, I go to the bathroom to freshen up.

"If you can put all of it over there and out of the way, that'd be great," I tell the young man.

"Is there anything else I can do for you, Mr. Keith?" in one last attempt to be of service.

"No, thank you, you did plenty," sending him on his way.

Man, oh man, let me tell you! When you go outside the gates and into the streets, people walking by will bump into you and think nothing of it. Not to mention, you have to be careful of all the rickshaws whizzing by. There are so many loud noises, as well as people everywhere wearing clothes of the loudest colors. There are shops, shops and more shops with hawkers that will tempt you to go in and spend money. And, all of this is done at an amazing speed. On top of all that, you have many people with illnesses, diseases, conditions and afflictions; it's truly the world in microcosm.

There are some people who wonder why Sai Baba doesn't do something about the poverty that's happening so near to Him. Those people in the streets know that those gates are always open for them, too. So the point is free will. Everyone has it now and forever, and if it takes a person forever to choose it, then so be it. That's the Law of Allowance in play. God doesn't force anything. As it was told to me by Spirit in my first book, *The Divine Principle*, "My reality is for those who really want it." We have to remember that Love isn't in a hurry or following a timepiece – Love is infinite.

People who try to dissect Baba into tiny bits could step back and see the Grand Scheme of what He has done, is doing and what He says He will do. There are many who worry that He is a scam artist, a charlatan, a child molester and the Antichrist. If one has the latter view, well, you can bet it all they've never read any books about Him and His life's message. For if they did, then they would be able see that no one but themselves is responsible for pigeon-holding them to a dogmatic, god-fearing religion or mindset.

God does not operate by this dynamic whatsoever. Why is

that so hard for people to get? In my opinion, fundamentalism can be seen as diseased when it comes to spirituality. Just about everyone in it believes to some degree only what they were told versus having experienced the truth that can only come from within one's own self. In return, they leave the evolution of their soul to blind faith. I just can't do that! I have to be involved. You have to be involved. We all have to be involved in order to truly grow.

On the way back to my room with Raahi, I saw a few people gathered around a vending stand in the courtyard that seemed interesting. I think I'll go check it out.

"Cool! A coconut juice stand."

"How much for one of those?" I ask a cross-eyed man wielding a big machete.

"Six rupees, Sai Ram."

"Great! I'll take one."

"Coming right up, Sai Ram," as he picks up a coconut, tosses it in the air a few times, whacks it with the machete, cutting the top off, sinks a tiny straw inside of it and hands it to me to gulp down. *"Boy, this is a nice treat!"* wiping the juice running down my face.

"Can I have another one?"

"Sure. But you must not drink anymore," as if to warn me.

"Why not?" I ask somewhat concerned.

"Because, too many of these and you will not be able to leave the toilet all day from a bad case of diarrhea," he tells me, laughing and revealing his lack of dental hygiene.

"Sai Ram, have you read any of the daily thoughts posted on the ashram yet?"

"No, I haven't," I reply.

"This is something you should do," he tells me, as he points down the way and moves on to the next customer.

Can you guess where I'm headed? Onward to read the thought boards, but I'll have to find them first. I'm thinking that these posts probably lay the groundwork for the lessons to be learned on any given day. And so, I'll log the insights into my recorder. This should be interesting.

"There it is!" I pick up my gait to hurry and check it out.

"Sai Ram," I say to greet a beautiful, earthy, long-brown-haired girl writing on the board.

As she turns to see me, I'm immediately overtaken by a subtle, yet powerful, angelic energy. *"Whoa!"* My heart chakra just burst wide open. Geez, Sweet Louise, let me tell you! Her eyes have a charge like lightning, so blinding and pure that it's making my kundalini (*sexual energy*) rise.

"Do you do this every day?" I ask the angel.

"Yes," she says, in a soft voice that somehow sounds off like a thunderclap. *"What's happening to me?"* I think to myself, as tears pour like rain from my eyes, along with my body flooding with many different emotions.

"If you don't mind me asking, how long have you been doing this?" barely getting the words out.

"Every day for the last four years," revealing her appreciation for the task.

Then with a genuflecting nod, smile and a wink, the angel "Sai Ram-s" me and walks away.

"Wow! What was that? Focus, Keith! Focus."

I need to pay attention to the reason I came to the board. It reads:

thought for the day
Be in perpetual contact with God.
Let the pipe that leads into the tap, which is you,
be connected with the reservoir of His Grace,
then your life will be full of unruffled content.
Without that awareness of the Constant Presence, any service
that you do to others will be dry, barren.
Be aware of It,

then any act of service will yield plentiful fruit.
Every person is a spark of the effulgence of God. God is
dancing in every cell of every being.
Do not doubt this.
Do not ignore this or dispute this!
This is the Truth! The entire Truth.
The only Truth.
The Universe is God. All this is He, His body.

*"I need to go and look for the other thought for the day board. I wonder
who I can ask to help me find it. Hmmm?"*

After walking around for a half hour, I now see the board
ahead of me. Here's what it says:

the other thought for the day
Understand that human birth
is the progeny of Truth
as the Father and Love as the Mother.
Even if one's natural parents are absent,
one should not forget the real parents,
Truth and Love.
When Truth and Love beget wisdom (Jnana),
as the son, the true lineage of man is established.
Truth is sacred; it is valued for all time;
past, present and future.
It is the unchanging. Love is eternal.
It is indescribably sweet, like nectar.
Can such Truth and Love
beget such an unrighteous and evil-minded child?
Only one who is wise and free from illusions
can be a true human being.

It's evening, and boy, what a great day this was for me! The
weather here was completely gorgeous and so was every soul I

encountered.

This place is literally Heaven on Earth. And, I can see how the beauty here on the ashram and what it stands for is what everyone seeks for fulfillment. As I recite these words into my recorder, it's hard for me to keep myself together from being so overwhelmed with it all. The contrast that exists between the inside and outside of the ashram is huge. Inside, all is in order, peaceful and flows nicely. On the outside, it's chaotic, loud and fast.

That's enough for now. I'm going to get some rest.

Deep Into the Rabbit Hole

Like yesterday, everyone on the ashram is up with the birds and marching with one eye open towards Kulwant Hall to sit in line and wait for darshan from Baba. I can sense that today is going to be spectacular.

"Keith, in that line, in that spot!" a voice from within says to me. Trusting and sitting where my intuition told me to, I pull out some cheese crackers to munch on to curb my hunger and pass the time.

Since I got to Kulwant Hall quite early, I find it somewhat humorous to see all the half-awake people show up, locate a spot and then drop like flies on the concrete for the next hour or so.

"Line 4, stand up. Line 10, stand up. Line 14, stand up. Line 9, stand up. Line 12, stand up. Line 7, stand up," says the man calling out the order.

"Line 7 … That's my line!"

After taking off my shoes (mandatory) outside the hall, I stop to admire the beauty of its exterior and feel fortunate to be here.

As I walk into the hall and through the metal detector, I open up full throttle to hurry and find that sweet spot where I will sit and wait for my Master. It still amazes me how people from all over the world come here in droves to experience God in the form of Sathya Sai Baba.

Shortly after finding my place in the first row, I notice the sounds of the parade approaching, and if every day in the ashram is the same, then I suspect that at any moment now, the huge, gold bell will sound and the twenty-one "Aum" chanting and Suprabhatam (whatever that is) will begin.

"Sai Ram?" says a young Indian man from behind me, tapping me on the shoulder.

"Yes?"

"When Lord Baba comes around us, do you mind if I reach over you to give Him a letter, asking if He would bless me and my concerns?"

"I'd love nothing more," I reply.

"Thank you, Sai Ram!" he says to me, then sits back down.

Yep! There it is. I'll definitely have to check out that Suprabhatam thing. "Baba, if it is Your will, lead me to it."

"BANG! – BANG! – BANG!" goes the bell, as we all begin to chant "Aum" twenty-one times to ask God to awaken and give us His darshan.

Now that the Hindi music is playing again, I'm sure Baba will be coming out as soon as it stops. This is still so exciting!

The music just stopped, and oh, my God, Sai Baba's now coming through the gate. Immediately, He goes to the women's side of the hall: talks to some, points to a few granting them an interview, materializes objects and collects letters. Even though Baba already knows what every letter says, He takes them anyway, giving all who have concerns the gift of feeling heard. I think that being acknowledged is much more important than what's actually in those letters they give Him.

Making His way over to the men's side, Baba does the same thing: blesses many, talks to some, points to a few for an interview, collects letters and materializes objects. Now He's making His way over to my area.

"Whoa!" Sai Baba is coming closer and I can feel His Light begin to engulf me. I know without a doubt this little man's reality is far beyond my ability to convey in a way that won't sully His sacredness.

Here He comes ... here He comes! Baba is upon me and His gown is brushing my arm.

"Excuse me, Sai Ram!" says the man from behind, as he leans on my shoulder for support to reach and give Sai Baba the letter that means so much to him. As Baba takes the letter from the young man, He never takes His eyes off him. Patting the letter in

His hand three times as if to check its content, Baba throws the letter back at the man saying, "You ought to know better than to give Me that! You put that where it belongs. There are proper channels in which to give what you are trying to give Me." Baba then walks off to finish His darshan.

"Sai Ram, what did you give Baba as to why He would throw the letter back to you like that?"

"I tried to give Him some money," he says, as he sits back down somewhat ashamed.

What in the world? Have I just witnessed Lord Baba in an Omniscient state? He actually knew what was in that envelope. It was like a Divine Script was written and acted out right in front of me. I mean, from the guy who asked to lean over my shoulder, to Baba walking up and touching me with His gown, then to experience the Master in His Omniscience. I was supposed to see that. That's why I knew my day was going to be spectacular. But what was most miraculous was, even though I heard everything Baba told the guy behind me, I don't recall Him speaking in English.

In the two days I've been here, so far, whenever Baba was near me, He manifested vibhuti ash. I'm not sure if that has any significance, so I think I'll not put too much into it and let things unfold.

Although Lord Baba is now finished with darshan and in the interview room with those lucky ones, I'm going to stay here in the hall to sing bhajans with the thousands that will remain here with me, too.

After singing for about thirty minutes, I can feel my energy continue to rise higher and higher with every song that we offer up in praise. But I'm starting to feel full. So, I think I'll enjoy the level of bliss I'm feeling and go explore the ashram some more.

"Where in the world are my shoes? I put them right here! Hmmm? I guess they'll reveal themselves after everyone in the hall collects theirs."

No such luck. Well, I guess that would be a good excuse for me to again step outside of the ashram to go buy some sandals.

As I walk through the gates, I notice a shop with many types of things; they'll probably have some sandals.

"Sai Ram. Can I help you?" asks the clerk.

"Yes, please. I'd like to buy those sandals (*pointing*)," I say to a short old man.

"Sit and try them out," he says.

Tugging on the straps, my feet say, "You can't be serious about this, can you?"

The clerk followed me outside laughing and saying, "They will stretch, but you have to wear them a lot."

Still, my feet say, "No, Keith, take them off!" "I think I will deal with it." I pay the man and walk back toward the ashram to look around and meet some folks.

After meeting people and hanging out in the courtyard for most of the morning, I look at my watch and realize that it's time for the afternoon darshan, and so, I'd better head toward Kulwant Hall.

Same as before: beautiful, graceful and full of love, Baba comes in and makes His way across the hall.

When I was in the courtyard a while ago, I decided that this afternoon when Sai Baba got close to where I was sitting, I'd hand Him the letters I had from friends, family and myself. Now, I just have to wait and hope that He comes close to me.

With Baba now on the men's side, I'm starting to feel somewhat nervous. Oh, oh! I've been spotted and Baba's coming straight toward me knowing I want to give Him something. This is so surreal!

As Baba takes the letters from me, in my mind I say to Him, "Thank You so much for everything in my life." Baba then gives me an intense look as if to look right through me. But I don't know if He's saying anything in particular with His eyes except that He's acknowledging my presence here on the ashram. I come to this conclusion because I'm looking at the Seva Dal next to me and his identification badge has my birthday on it.

Ten minutes or so go by, and after He points to a few more people to go to the back room for their interview, Baba and the lucky ones disappear behind the door.

Looking for my new sandals ... *"There's one ... and yes, there's the other."* But my feet were hoping that they wouldn't be found.

Oh, I forgot to tell you, this morning when I lost my tennis shoes, an old lady saw me searching and came over and told me, "Someone taking your shoes means that the bad luck in you has dissipated. But, let me tell you of your good luck that begins now with a foolproof way to hang on to them from here on out. The best thing to do is separate them so that only you know where they are." This seems simple, but effective. After putting my new sandals on and after few good tugs on the straps, I assure my feet that everything would soon be alright.

As I begin my walk around the ashram for the rest of the afternoon, I'm going over in my head whether or not I was purposely placed on the first row to experience what transpired between Baba and the man that sat behind me in Kulwant Hall.

You might be thinking, "Boy, that Keith sure does process a lot." Well, yes, I do. In fact, every day ... all day long. Most spiritualists won't, or even can't for that matter, shut this "processing" off. Like those others, my habit to consciously connect is so powerful it consumes me. I guess you can call me a God addict.

I think today is about me realizing how being here is awakening me to higher aspects of myself, while revealing the lower ones so I can finally resolve them.

After walking around the ashram for quite a while, I'm back in my room and hanging out with Damiere.

"Keith, my brother in Sai, today when I was out and about, I saw something in one of the shops that made me think of you.

I bought it hoping that, maybe some time when you meditate, you would sit on it and think of me," he said as he hands me a beautiful, decorative rug.

"Damiere, I'm so touched by your gift … thank you!" I say with tears in my eyes, as I head to the balcony to get some fresh air.

"Hey, Mister, would you come down and play ball with me?" asks a little Asian boy of about seven years old.

"Sure! I'll be right there."

"Damiere, would you like to come with me to play with this child? Maybe after that, we can go to the thought for the day board."

"Sure. Let's go be kids again," he replies laughing.

"Hello, my name is Elijah! What's yours?" he says in a British accent.

"I'm Keith."

"Hi, Mr. Keith."

"Hi, Mr. Elijah," acknowledging his adult-like ways.

"Oh, wow … this boy is bright!" Baba must have placed him here for me to see the God-fire burning within him. Damiere is also consumed by the boy.

Tossing the ball back and forth between the three of us, it seems to be a challenge for me to catch it, because I can't stop staring at the light that is emanating from Elijah. I'm so wrapped up in this kid's energy that, this time when he threw the ball to me, my not paying attention landed it right on top of my head. I guess I'm supposed to be the butt of Baba's joke because everyone is laughing, including me.

"Elijah! Come inside, son. It's time to eat, clean up and rest for the night," says a man that appears to be the boy's father. I walk up to his parents and tell them what a great child they are raising. "He is not like most kids," his mom says. "He is one who lives in the favor and grace of Baba." And, after a brief encounter, we all bless each other with a "Sai Ram" and go about our separate ways.

As Damiere and I walk toward the thought boards, we chat a bit about the magic we just experienced with Elijah.

"The first one is right down here," I tell Damiere.

"I know where it is, Keith. I have been here for four months. But you know what?" he asks.

"What's that?"

"I think I will only do one thought board today. After that, I am going to go back to the room to do a bunch of nothing. Would you like to go do that with me?"

"Sure."

thought for the day
You need to know
the answers to two questions only.
Who is Baba and who am I?
And the answer is:
I am the reflected image of Baba.
Baba is the original
of which I am the reflection.
That is the relationship – that is the bond.
Whether you know it or not –
whether the image is distorted or correct.
You do meditation morning and evening.
You do prayer beads.
You engage yourself in all kinds of worship
all for realizing that you are but an image
to become a clean, clear image of the Lord.
So clean and clear that you merge in Him.

Back at the room, Damiere and I are about to get some rest. But, before I hit the hay, I think I'll meditate on this insightful day.

Today was awesome in that, as Baba took the letters from me and looked me in the eyes, it became abundantly clear He was showing me depth. It felt like He was taking me into a rabbit hole where I could feel my connection to Him on a deeper level. Though there was no expression on His face other than calmness, the Presence I could feel from Him was truly amazing! And while Baba was in my section, I reached to touch His feet, but couldn't quite get to them. So, I figure today wasn't the day. But at least I was able to thank Him for the many wonderful things He has blessed me with.

There's so much I'm absorbing that I'm wondering how I will ever go about processing it all. Maybe this is not a "try to" kind of thing. Maybe it's a "let blossom" kind of thing, and that it will take years for the seeds being planted to germinate.

Swinging Back and Forth

*Today feels to be about expansion. "Why am I up so early?" stretching
my arms and letting out a big yawn. After I make my way over to the
bathroom for a quick groom, I hit the door running …*

*"… Why am I running down the street and where am I going? It
seems that my feet know, but I don't."*

"Sai Ram! Why are you running so fast and where are you
going?" asks one of two men sitting on the curb.

"I have no clue," I reply, feeling somewhat lost in a dream.

"We know," says the other one smiling.

"How do these people seem to know everything?"

"Come … sit here," says the first man.

"Thanks, Sai Ram. Why are you both waiting here and what's
in that room?" I ask panting.

"We are waiting here for Suprabhatam that will happen in
there," says both of them together.

"Suprabhatam … yes, this is it!"

"I was told by someone else that Baba would lead me here if
I asked Him. Is it a cool experience?"

"It is very cool! Your journey to the ashram would not be
complete unless you came to this," says the second man.

"Very soon people will begin to flood the streets going to
Kulwant Hall. You came at the right time, Sai Ram," says the
first man.

"How long do we wait before we go inside?"

"We will wait here for about an hour," replies the first man.

"Do you both mind if I lean against this wall and get a little
shut eye?" I ask them out of respect.

"Sai Ram, what?" asks the second man confused.

"Would you mind if I got some sleep until it's time go in?" I
say, realizing they didn't understand my lingo.

"Oh, no, go ahead, Sai Ram," they say in unison.

About an hour later ...

"Sai Ram. You might want to wake up now. People are starting to get in line. It won't be long before we go into the room for Suprabhatam," says the first man.

Wiping my eyes, I stand up and brush the dirt from my derriere.

"Everyone, come ... this way. Shhh ... no talking ... and don't look at the women! You will sit on one side while they sit on the other. No distractions," says the man who just opened the door to let all of us in.

In a single-file line thirty or so men begin to pile into the small room.

Taking my seat, I begin to look around. *"Whoa ... this is amazing!" not believing what I'm seeing and feeling.* Not only am I fortunate to experience Lord Baba in the ashram, I'm blessed to experience the Godhead (Temple) in physical form. Again, this is where mere words only soil the Sacred. Everything in this Temple is the Holiest of Holy and has been seen by only a few. So, in this moment, I'm feeling like one very blessed man.

Inside this room there's an actual chariot and a real-life statue of a beautiful white horse. There are also large pictures of Krishna, Arjuna, Baba of Shirdi and Sathya Sai Baba that don the walls – fragrant flowers everywhere. *"There's no place more sacred than this on the face of the Earth!" I say to myself.*

In this room, the Divine energy is so palpable that it almost "hurts" to look upon anything when my mind is chattering. And, it seems the only way I can see anything clearly is when I go within and humble myself.

Musicians begin to play and everyone in the room begins to sing. Since I don't know the words or what's going on, I'll wait to learn the melody and hum on the next round.

After about fifteen minutes of music and singing, it all slowly softens until everything becomes completely still; filled with a silence I've never experienced in my life.

"BANG! – BANG! – BANG!" sounds the golden bell, and just like that, 35,000 souls in Kulwant Hall begin to chant twenty-one "Aums."

"Oh, My God! What's happening?" It feels like the Breath of God is moving through me, as this little room and my heart begin to resonate like a tuning fork. I can't seem to describe it, except that I hear this loud buzzing sound and see bright light. But there's something else and I have no idea what it is. My physical body seems to be disappearing; like it is melting away, revealing my Soul Essence. I'm in such awe and humility that I can feel my connection to the entire universe. And, now that there's no inner distortion, I can see everything in here perfectly, too!

When the last of the twenty-one "Aums" are chanted, it's over ... just like that!

"Everyone, get up. It's time to leave. Shhh ... no talking!" says the man who opened the door to let us in.

I can't begin to describe what happened in there. In fact, the only thoughts I'm having, I'm logging into my tape recorder. But I can tell you that I'm feeling blissful and overwhelmed.

"Is this only a glimpse of what true enlightenment is?"

Because I just attended Suprabhatam, I'll have to sit in the back for Lord Baba's appearance. I don't mind because I know that what just transpired is far greater for my growth than being in close proximity to Him.

Settling into my spot I notice the gentleman next to me reading a book.

"Sai Ram, what are you reading and who is it by?" I ask.

"Here ... take a look," he says, showing me the cover.

"Oh, my Goodness gracious! The author's name is Kenneth Blanchard." As soon as I realize we have the exact surname, a

voice from within tells me, "Keith, be aware and do not take your eyes off of Me for a second. I will do two things, but you must be watching!"

As the days before, Indian music and a murmuring mass fill the air, until God graces us with His Presence. When the music stops, everyone becomes silent and all heads and attention turn toward the gate. Entering the hall and walking from the women's to the men's side, Baba takes letters, talks and points to a few, manifests objects and blesses us all.

While I was home in Memphis, I decided that I'd wait for just the right moment to ask Baba whether or not I should complete the book I've been working on for four years titled *The Divine Principle: Anchoring Heaven On Earth*. I don't know if I should continue writing it or put my energy into something else. And so, I figured Baba would tell me what to do and that, whatever answer He would give me, I'll accept and be happy with. *"This has to be the perfect time to ask Him what to do."*

With Baba as near as He will be today, I ask from my heart, "If You want me to continue writing this book, give me the same sign You gave Robert Priddy which he told of in his book, *Source of the Dream*." In it, Baba told Robert in a personal interview: "When I pointed to you and wrote in the air with my finger, that was a sign that I want you to write a book about my life and what you experience here on the ashram."

No sooner than I ask Baba to give me the same sign that He gave Robert, lo' and behold, Baba stops what He is doing, turns around and begins to look at me all the way in the back. *"Surely Baba's not looking at me from that distance. It makes more sense for Him to do that when He's closer."* Then it dawns on me ... *"That's the point entirely; His peeking through the all rows of people is to show me that it's deliberate."* Three steps later, Sai Baba comes from behind all the people to an opening where there is no obstruction in our line of sight.

All of a sudden, His hand goes up as He begins to write in

the air. I'm freaking out! So much so that I'm putting my face in my hands with disbelief of what's happening. *"I wonder if He will do it again?" I say to myself.*

"Lord Baba, please give me the same sign again to show me that You are answering my question." Removing my hands from my face and looking up, *"Oh, my God!"* His hand is writing in the air again. Now, I'm really starting to freak! *"One time, wow! Two times, really wow! Three times? Yeah, three times! That's the magic number and I'm going to go for it."*

"Baba, shall I continue writing the book and publish it?" Up His hand goes yet again, looking directly at me through the crowd with those eyes as if to say, "You heard Me now, Keith!" Baba then turns down the final stretch of His path toward the little room where He will grant the lucky ones an interview.

Leaving Kulwant Hall and walking toward the thought for the day boards, I have no doubt whatsoever that Baba spoke to me.

"But how do you know that for sure, Keith?" you might ask. Because something inside tells me so. It's a feeling of rightness, goodness and alignment that reverberates within me surrounding the completion of *The Divine Principle*.

The way Baba answered me about finishing the book was not only by writing in the air. It was also through the alignment of my shared surname with that author, telling me He wanted my name on a book cover, too.

"Whoa ... that's amazing!" as yet another revelation comes to me. My father has a brother named Kenneth Blanchard who happens to be my "God"-father!

It's obvious that grace and miracles are present everywhere in the ashram and should answer the question about, "How do you know for sure that Sai Baba talked to you?" I guess I'll go check out the thought boards.

thought for the day
I want to tell you that the bliss you derive
from service is something you can
never get from any other activity.
The thrill that a kind word,
a small gift, a good gesture,
a sigh of sympathy, a sign of compassion
can bring about on a distressed heart
is something that is beyond words to describe.

Back in my room, I realize how much I like reading the daily thoughts and for two reasons: to see how my day correlates to its message and hoping to meet up with the angel who writes them.

Lying on the bed, I'm going through some books and I found a few good insights.

The first one is:

"The yogis should be looked upon as friends and good qualities should be regarded as true kinsmen. Yoga does not consist of meditation and austerities or various forms of breath control.

True yoga is the mergence of the senses from external objects and turning them inwards. To allow the senses free rein is not yoga but sensual enjoyment. Such indulgence only leads to disease. Yoga implies self-control and renunciation, leading to the experience of ongoing bliss."

The second one is:

"Do not ask another what state you belong to or which caste or creed you profess. See your favorite form of God in that other person. As a matter of fact, He is not other at all. It is his image as much as you are his. You are not helping some one individual. You are adoring Me in him. I am before you in that form. So what room is there for the ego in you to raise its hood?"

Since I've been here, I've noticed that, whenever I'm sitting down like now, I catch myself rocking back and forth. Yesterday, I asked Lord Baba to show me something that would explain why I'm doing this.

Immediately upon asking Him, Wendy who I mentioned earlier in the book came to mind. Whenever I was around her, I noticed that she would do this rocking thing all the time. I guess I, like she, am riding an energy that comes into the body.

*Something is telling me to put this book down and grab another one from my bag (*Inner Dialogue With Sai Baba*) and open it randomly. After doing so, this is what I found.*

"When the soul is no longer stained from the protecting sheaths, the indwelling Divinity can be brought out. Only then can the Shiva's power be put into operation. That power is effective only when there is a complete understanding of what one is doing.

Becoming Divine is an intuitive process of a pure heart. Shiva power is a process of the whole integrated consciousness where all qualities/talents are used optimally once the heart is pure and the nature sanctified.

Following a later continuation of this dream which there is talk of Sai Baba on a swing, note that on special occasions Baba sits on a beautifully decorated swing. He says this is how we should feel Him in our hearts, swinging gently back and forth."

My, that answer came quickly! There's such an alignment and order here that nothing struggles to be.

But what I really want to know is, why am I eating so darn much? Is it a cosmic thing? Does it represent sustenance on all levels?

Amen To That!

I'm about to collect my things and start my morning walk towards Kulwant Hall for darshan.

It just occurred to me that, every day I'm here, my pace down to Kulwant Hall slows. I guess I'm starting to realize that no matter what time you get to the concrete waiting area, it has no effect whatsoever on where you are going to sit for darshan, because where everyone sits is orchestrated by Baba. I know it may be hard to believe that there's a Being here on Earth today that has the power to be able to do such things. But, if you look back into scriptural history, they all speak of Avatars (Divine Descents) that would come with Divine powers to lift mankind out of its self-created quagmire.

Sathya Sai Baba is regarded by other Avatars as the Highest Incarnation of God to ever come to the planet. This is in no way implying that one God being is better or higher than the other. It's from the perspective that Baba is the Godhead manifested as human, compared to Jesus and Buddha who over the course of their lives "became" God. Though many Avatars are imbued with spiritual awareness and power, it's Baba's Divinity that is the point being made here.

After making my way to the slab and dropping down on my bottom, I wait to go into the hall. Suddenly, I notice what appears to be a thirteen-year-old boy waving at me from across the way.

"Who me?" I pantomime and point to myself.

"Yes, yes! I will see you inside the hall," he mouths, while nodding.

"What in the world could he possibly want with me?"

After waiting about an hour, they are now starting to call out the lines to march us into Kulwant Hall.

"Line 5, stand up, please," says the man with a clipboard.

"Hey ... that's my line and we are first!"

Placing my sandals near the hall entrance, I walk through the metal detector and race as fast as I can to find a sweet spot. Settled into what I think is the best seat in the house, I look around at the architectural marvel that is the Kulwant Hall. It's so beautiful! The ceilings are made of gold imported from Thailand, while the design was crafted with devotion, love and care. Everything was taken into consideration during its creation, so as to be a place worthy of worshipping the Divine. I could stay in here and never leave, and be happy for the rest of my life.

Pulling out some cheesy crackers to munch on, I notice that same little boy waving at me from across the way with excitement, as if to say that he has something for me. I wave back at him saying, "Okay ... thanks!"

"I wonder where this could possibly be leading? It has to mean something," I say to myself.

I'm a big believer in that there're no coincidences, and surely, not here in the ashram. I guess it will unfold when it does.

"BANG! – BANG! – BANG!" sounds the gold bell, as we fall into the twenty-one chants. Closing my eyes, I begin, "Aum ... Aum ... Aum ... Aum." All of a sudden, I'm seeing that excited little boy waving at me in my mind's eye. *"There's no telling if this kid is illumined beyond what I'm giving him credit for and is actually here with me in this way. I guess I should wave back."*

I'm floored when I open my eyes to find just that. Maybe this is what he was trying to tell me outside of the hall; that he was going to pop into my mind and make contact. *"I wonder if there's more to come with this kid."*

The Hindi music just turned off and so that must mean Baba's about to walk into the hall. And, there He is, but today, He's wearing a blood-red robe. In all my experiences with Baba, I have always seen Him wearing orange: in dreams, in pictures and even here on the ashram. Maybe I need to find out the significance of the different colored robes.

As before, Lord Baba walks into the hall and gives His full attention to the women's side, taking their heartfelt letters, chatting with some, manifesting things and pointing to the lucky ones for an interview.

Making His way over to the men's side, I'm filled with excitement and anticipation, wondering if Baba will lay eyes on me today. Well, what do you know? The little boy is waving at me again. *"Is something miraculous about to happen and is that boy trying to tell me so?"*

With Baba near me, I ask Him in my thoughts if there's anything significant about this boy playing with me. Upon finishing my question, Baba looks at me and begins to wave just like the boy did and with the same excitement.

In this moment, I'm filled with feelings of expansion and validation, but also with a knowing that everything happening with this kid points to now. Strangely, it feels like I'm waking up from a foggy dream and thrown into a hyper-conscious reality, and somehow, that boy is the door.

With a final wave and a nod, Baba turns down another aisle to bless the other men and eventually disappears into the room to give interviews.

After singing bhajans for about an hour, I'm leaving the hall to find something to eat. As I step outside the ashram gate to grab some fresh fruit, guess who's standing there waving at me? Yes ... the boy! With so many questions, I walk up to him.

"Do you speak English?"

"Not really, Sai Ram," patting me on my chest, as he turns and walks away waving.

Taking it all in while getting some fruit from a lady vendor, I decide to head toward the daily thought boards, thinking it may shed some light on my morning with this magical boy.

thought for the day
The yogis should be looked upon as friends

and good qualities should be
regarded as true kinsmen.
Yoga does not consist of
meditation and austerities
or various forms of breath control.
True yoga is the mergence of the senses
from external objects and turning them inwards.
To allow the senses free rein is not yoga
but sensual enjoyment.
Such indulgence will lead to disease.
Yoga implies self-control and renunciation,
leading to the experiencing of bliss.

Oh, wow! I wrote that same thought toward the end of the last chapter. *"I wonder what the connection is."*

the other thought for the day
Do not ask another what state you belong to
or which caste or creed you profess.
See your favorite form of God
in that other person.
As a matter of fact, He is not other at all.
It is his image as much as you are.
You are not helping some one individual.
You are adoring Me in him. I am before you in that form.
So what room is there for the ego in you
to raise its hood?

After spending the day walking around meeting people, I'm finally in my room and settled for bed. Going over all that happened earlier, I can't help but think of the magic between the boy, Baba and myself, wondering how the thoughts for the day relate to it all.

Likened to the first thought board, the little boy is a friend and a yogi (someone who is self-realized) and was trying to tell me to dwell more in the heart to bypass my senses to reach a state of bliss.

Like the second daily thought board said, I never should've asked him if he spoke English. By doing so, I insinuated that we were somehow different. I created a division between us by not seeing nor believing that he and I are connected through Baba as the Bridge. When the boy patted me on the chest, I knew it was significant and the realization for it was soon to come – which is now. Amen to that!

What A Great Day To Be Alive!

It's 4:42am, and I'm headed toward Kulwant Hall, to sit among the tens-of-thousands as we await blessings from the Highest Incarnation of God to have ever walked on the Earth.

After sitting on the slab for about fifteen minutes, I find myself still wanting to be seen or talked to by Baba. I will have to find a way to release this in order see Him more clearly within.

What I *should* do when this "I want an interview" thought and feeling comes is redirect my focus by placing all that happens in Baba's hands. So, instead of, "I want an interview," I could say, "Sit me where I need to sit for my highest good." I'm thinking that this mantra should dilute any trace of my wanting and give me more of the outcome I truly desire anyway.

"Line 16 ... please stand up. Let's go!" said the man with the clipboard.

After separating my sandals and hiding them outside the hall, I make my way through the metal detector and run to find my place. *"Yes ... third row!"*

From my prime piece of real estate, I'm watching the Seva Dals roll out red carpet that I assume Baba will walk on as He meanders through the mass of people. *"What is that? Oh, cool!"* There are lotus petals engraved on the carpet about every three feet. Why haven't I noticed this before, even when I was on the first row? *"I wonder if that has any significance."*

"BANG! – BANG! – BANG!" sounds the bell, as we chant twenty-one "Aums," asking God to awaken.

Without fail, several minutes later, Baba walks through the gate and blesses everyone with His Love. The people here are so strong in their devotion that their lives become ones of constant prayer for the betterment of themselves and their loved ones. This seems to be the sustenance that feeds the entire ashram.

Sai Baba has made the final turn and then goes into the interview room with the lucky ones.

As I exit the hall, I remember that, yesterday, I read a flyer that was posted saying one of Baba's personal assistants would be giving a talk today after darshan. I think I'll go check it out.

The lecture room is packed with people wall-to-wall and the temperature is off the chart. The three ceiling fans spinning are making very little difference. As I look around, I see everyone fanning themselves with whatever they can find to move a little more air.

"Hello and welcome to today's talk about my time with Baba as His personal assistant," says an older Indian man with a thick accent.

"Today, I will share with you many things about Baba and will take any questions at the end of my presentation.

I have spent many years with my Baba ever since we were children. But my time being of service to Him has developed into something far beyond friendship or measure."

For an hour, on and on the man went about some of the most phenomenal stories I've ever heard about Baba's Love, Magic and Power.

"If there are any questions from the audience, I will take them now," he said.

Of course, my hand goes up like an excited schoolboy in class.

"Yes, Sai Ram. What is your question?"

"I've been wrestling with something for a couple of days now. Whenever I leave the ashram and go out into the streets ..."

"... Why are you leaving the ashram, Sai Ram? That is not recommended!" he interrupts, while giving me a stern look.

"Personal reasons," I reply.

"You should not mix and mingle with the beggars and others out there!" he says, as if to scold me. "What is your question?"

"My question is about compassion. Whenever I go out of the ashram, my heart hurts because of my want to help others. What is your advice about what to do in a situation like this, be it here on the ashram or anywhere else for that matter?" I ask, hoping to get the answer that will alleviate my ache.

"As I said, you should not go out of the ashram ever because ..."

On and on the man went in a fussing-like way, leaving me with nothing to satisfy my desire to be of service.

"Sai Ram?" says an African man from behind, tapping me on the shoulder.

"Yes, Sai Ram?"

"Your desire to want to help others is enough," he says to me, sitting back down in his spot.

"Thank you, my brother!" I say to him with tears in my eyes and feeling complete with my dilemma.

After about ten or so more questions from the audience, the presentation is over. I think now is the perfect time to hit the thought for the day boards to see if they shed more light on the question I put to Baba's assistant.

Coming down the final stretch to the first thought board, again I notice just how beautiful it is here. There are so many flowers, plants, trees, birds and people from all walks of life and in every color, coexisting in a way that's truly Divine.

thought for the day
Your service to man is more valuable
than what you call service to God.
God has no need of your service.
You please man. You please God.
The Purusha Suktha sings of God as having
a thousand heads, a thousand eyes
and a thousand feet.
That is to say, all beings are He.
They are not separate!
Note that it is not mentioned that

He has a thousand hearts.
There is only one heart.
The same blood circulates through all heads and hands.
When you tend the limb, you tend the individual.
When you serve man, you serve God!

the other thought for the day
You owe a supreme duty towards your parents
who are responsible for all that you are.
You have to strive constantly to please them.
If you don't show your gratitude to the parents
who have brought you up
with so much love and labor,
to whom else are you going to be grateful?
You must cultivate a broad heart and develop love towards all
beings as emblems of the Divine.
You have to live up to the upanishadic injunctions
to regard your mother, father, guru
and guest as God.
Your love should not be based
only the physical forms.
Bodies are perishable and impermanent.

I love reading the thought boards. More often than not, they relate to what's going on and are helpful in processing the events for any given day.

I think I'll go find my roommate and hang out with him for a while.

After looking in the room and a few other places to find Damiere, I finally catch up with him in the courtyard where he is talking to a few people by the coconut stand, drinking one of those drinks.

"Sai Ram, can I please get one of those?" I ask a man with little teeth.

"Six rupees, Sai Ram," he says, as he tosses one up in the air, catches it, whacks the top off, slides a straw in it and hands it to me.

"Brother Keith, what are you going to do with the rest of your day?" asks Damiere.

"I was thinking about going out of the ashram to see the house and the village where Baba grew up."

"You are not supposed to go beyond the gates!" he tells me with a smile.

"Damiere ... are you telling me that, after all the time you've been here, you've never left the ashram?" laughing, knowing that he has and still does. "Do you want to go with me?"

"I've done that many times. Have fun!" he said.

I head out the gates only to be prompted back in by a strong intuition ... "Keith, go to the courtyard to just sit and be still until the second darshan takes place."

I'm last to arrive at the slab where everyone waits to be called into the hall for darshan.

"Sit there, in line 8," an intuitive voice tells me.

"Line 7, stand up!" yells the man with the clipboard.

As the last person in line 7 stands up and marches toward Kulwant Hall, I find myself standing up, too, as if I'm supposed to follow.

"You are in line 8 ... not 7! Please sit down, Sai Ram."

As I take my seat, a voice from within says to me, "Keith, you are next."

"Line 8, please stand up," says the same man, all the while looking at me with a smile on his face.

I'm overjoyed for the chance to see Baba up close yet again and for being aligned with my intuitive voice.

After leaving my sandals outside and clearing the metal detector, I find myself squatting down on the second row and I'm very pleased.

"What's that ... a better place?" I get up and off I jet across the aisle where a first-row spot just became available. Halfway there, someone a little faster than I beat me to it. I was happy for him. On my way back to my original spot on the second row, a Seva Dal yells to me, "Over there!" pointing to a prime location. I move to that spot and squat on the first row with a sense of victory. *"Yes!"*

After sitting here a while in prayer and meditation, the Seva Dal who found me this sweet spot comes up to me and asks, "Sai Ram, have you ever had the honor of kissing Sai Baba's feet?"

"For the love of God, no."

"Maybe today is your lucky day," he says to me, as if knowing that that is going to happen. I begin to dwell on how awesome it would be if it did.

It's about 2:15pm with Baba now in Kulwant Hall. As always, He starts by blessing the women's side and by the time He reaches the men's, He will have blessed many thousands.

With Baba now near, He looks directly at me wearing a soft smile, as if to say, "I am pleased with you, Keith, for all your passionate, hard work to become a better human being."

"Oh, my God!" Baba's walking straight toward me ... closer and closer and closer. So close that, I have to look up to see His face. But when I look down, His little feet are right there! I'm suddenly overwhelmed knowing that all the events that led to this moment are by Sai Baba's design. In appreciation, humility and love, I lean over to kiss my beloved Lord's feet, the whole time saying to Him, "Thank you for my life and the opportunity to come into my own Divinity."

As I pull up from kissing and touching Baba's feet, I'm filled with such joy and blessedness that I begin to cry profusely. I'm flabbergasted about how this entire event has played out like a script: from the beginning of getting into line, to this moment of realization. Again, I find myself in the space and magic of no time. What a great day to be alive!

With afternoon darshan now over and feeling hungry, I recall that Damiere told me earlier to make sure I try the vegetarian pizza they make at the little store in the ashram. Bet you know where I'm going.

Wow … mmmm … the pizza is soooo good! It has tomatoes, onions, garlic and whatever else, I can't seem to stop eating it. I'm sure that my ongoing hunger *has* to be a sign of being open and ready to receive sustenance.

As I sit down to eat my last slice, I'm thinking about kissing Baba's feet in the hall. And, I feel it's important that I become silent for the rest of the day to integrate and further expand into the gift of which I was blessed.

At this point on my sojourn, I can feel my intuition increasing evermore. It's like there is a furnace burning in my heart and in my head.

Stoking the Fire Within

Today's a good day to just chill out with no distractions.

I'll probably hang in the courtyard, visit the daily thought boards and maybe wander around later to take in some new sites. It's beneficial to be able to balance, digest and process everything I've taken in up to this point. But, I'm still very hungry!

thought for the day
Love can beget only through love.
A different path of devotion like santhi (peace),
sathya (friendship), batsalia (material love),
anuraga (affection), madhura marga (sweetness),
are all based on love.
The essence of spiritual discipline is contained in love.
The greater a man's love for God,
the greater is the bliss which he experiences!
When love declines in man,
his joy also declines equally.
The lover of God sees God everywhere.
Hence, man's heart must be filled
with the love of God.

the other thought for the day
Know that seva (service) is a better form of
discipline than even meditation.
How can God appreciate the meditation you do
when adjacent to you, you have someone in agony who you do
not treat kindly.
For whom you do not make all effort to help.
Do not keep yourself apart intent on your own salvation
through prayer beads or meditation.

Move among your systems
looking for opportunities to be of help.
But have the name of God on the tongue
and the form of God before the eye of the mind.
That is the highest spiritual discipline;
Ram on the heart, task on the hand.
Proceed in that spirit.
Grace will be showered on you in full measure.

After an easy, relaxed day, I'm headed back to my room to cut up some cards for a new device I purchased.

Just a bit ago, I attended a very insightful class about a powerful healing system called Vibrionics. Dr. Aggarwal, the instructor, told us this method of healing was like no other. But, before I could take his class, I had to vow that I would never charge future patients money for my practice. Because in doing so, the intention would be for profit, not for healing. When the good doctor told me this, I was filled with an absolute knowing of how this method would change the lives of many sick people.

Making my way to the entrance that leads up to my room, I notice a small crowd gathered at the bottom of the stairway.

"Sai Ram, but what's going on here?" I ask a gentleman who seems to know.

(*Pointing*) "Look ... see for yourself! There is a lot of vibhuti ash falling off Sai Baba and Mother Mary's picture hanging on the wall!" said the man with great excitement.

"Whoa ... that's amazing!"

There's holy ash spontaneously manifesting from these two pictures and falling onto spiritual figurines sitting on the floor just below, almost covering them. Believe me when I tell you, to see something like this creates a shift inside. It's nothing like I've ever seen. I was told when I got to the ashram that I'd likely see this phenomenon. I was also told that, whatever I do, do not touch the pictures from which it was happening because it would stop the manifesting process.

"Sai Ram?" says a young Oriental lady.

"Yes?"

"Here ... this is a gift for you," as she bends down to scoop up some ash from the figurines. "Put some of it in your mouth and treat it as a blessing from God. Notice the warmth and how it tastes like flowers," she says with much delight in her gift to me. So, I put some on my forehead and the rest went into my mouth.

"Oh, my God!" It tastes even better than she described; like something spontaneously created by God would. Going down my throat, I can feel the holy ash as if it were Divine bellows stoking the fire within. No more words. No more words.

Thank You, Grace!

You know the routine by now. It's around 4:15 in the morning and I'm on my way to the concrete slab to wait to be called into Kulwant Hall.

"Line 10, please stand up. Line 15, stand up. Also, lines 1, 8, 4, 9 and 12, stand up and move toward the hall," says the man with the clipboard. *"Here we go!"*

Removing my sandals and going through the metal detector, I find myself sitting on the third row enjoying the idea that others have the opportunity to get close to Baba.

After the morning parade, Hindi music and the ringing of that bell, Sai Baba's coming through the gate. As always, He starts on the women's side by collecting letters, healing some, pointing to a few along the way granting them an interview and materializing different things.

Baba's now on the men's side of the hall and is manifesting from His hand gobs of ash all around us. Wow! It seems so natural for Him to do this. He's approaching an older gentleman while readying some more ash to give to him. There's so much flowing, the devotee can't contain it all. People in proximity are like buzzards or hyenas moving in for the scraps that hit the floor. I'm in such awe from the Divinity and spontaneous will that pour out from this Avatar. Sai Baba turns down the final aisle and heads into the interview room to talk with the lucky ones.

In the last few days I've really opened myself up. I know without a doubt that my experience here in the ashram with Baba will shave years off of my spiritual work. Thank you, Grace! Back to the thought boards I go.

thought for the day
Love will not enter the heart of one
who is filled with selfishness and self-conceit.

Therefore, man should forget his petty self
and concentrate his thoughts on God.
Love of God makes a man
oblivious of his own existence.
Love becomes a form of intoxication.
Love makes the devotee and God
dance in ecstasy and becomes one with him.
It induces self-forgetfulness.
It generates an ecstasy in which
everything is forgotten.

the other thought for the day

The foremost task today is to
get rid of the pride and other demonical qualities by leading a
pure and sacred life.
This is not a single act, but a process.
The right action you do today
by repetition becomes a ritual.
Today's ritual becomes tomorrow's habit
and the habit in due course
becomes a spiritual discipline.
Spiritual discipline leads to your life's goal.
Hence, the realization of the goal
depends on your action.

Today, I'll again step outside the ashram to finalize my gift and
souvenir buying. But I have to remember to surround myself
with light to protect me from the lower energies that can latch
on. You do understand that my whole purpose of going out is
healing, right? I mean, I want to buy saris, japamalas, pictures
of Baba; anything to transform my little apartment into a shrine
dedicated to Baba's Divine Love. I'm so humbled that I want to
always/all ways remember my precious time here in India, the
ashram and those I've met. That's a good thing, right? So, out

of the Gates of Heaven I go and into the streets where money becomes lord.

Just leaving the ashram, I'm having a serious case of déjà vu. This is the third one this week. It's not normal to have that many in such a short amount of time. Again, this reveals the kind of alignment one falls into when in the ashram.

Back in my room from shopping, I remember that a few days ago, I asked Sai Baba in prayer to help me find someone I could share a taxi with back to Bangalore. I could use the good company for the four-hour trip, as well as save a few dollars.

Just a bit ago, I saw a sign someone posted with regards to carpooling. So, I'm headed toward their room to meet them and to see if we can make the shared ride happen.

"Hello … Sai Ram?" (*knocking on the door*)

"Hmmm? No one's answering. I guess I'll head to the courtyard to get me one of those scrummy, yummy drinks for a big whopping six rupees."

"Sai Ram? Hello," I say to this tiny, illumined lady upon arriving at the coconut stand.

"Do you know how to select the best coconut?" she asks in a foreign accent.

"I sure do. I was enlightened about that the other day by one of the gentlemen who works here. What's your name?" I ask.

"My name is Ana and I'm from Yugoslavia."

"I'm Keith," extending out my hand for a shake and asking her, "How long have you been here in the ashram and how long are you staying?"

"I've been here for two weeks now and will be headed back home this Sunday."

"That's the same day I'm heading back home."

"Are you going to go by taxi?" I ask in the hope that she says, "Yes."

"No. I'm flying out from the little airport down the street.

Why do you ask?"

"I'm trying to find someone to carpool back to Bangalore."

"Sorry, I can't. But my Aunt Rasa is going back to Bosnia via Bangalore and maybe you can share the ride. The information of where to find me (*pointing*) is posted on that wall over there."

"Wow! I just came from your room hoping to meet you and here you are. Well, isn't that something?"

"Isn't it, though?" she says to me with a big smile.

"Sai Ram, can I invite you to my room later to meet my Aunt Rasa and participate in a Puja session (*an act of showing reverence to God*)?"

"Of course ... I'd love nothing more."

"Come ... follow me," she says, wiggling her finger and walking in the direction of her room.

The Puja session with Ana and Rasa was special. The prayer, the meditation and the ritual of drinking blessed rose water was the perfect ending to a most magnificent day. Now it's bedtime for Bonzo.

Apply, Integrate, Transcend, Be

This morning I didn't go to darshan. I'm starting to feel that I need to chill out more; like I'm doing too much. So, I think today I'll stay in my room, do some more writing, and maybe later, if I can find the energy, visit the thought boards.

Believe it or not, I feel homesick. I actually appreciate this feeling because I see how much I love Memphis, all my friends and the life I have there. Nonetheless, when I see Sai Baba, not only does it make me feel better, it makes my heart pound in my chest … still!

Reflecting on the life I lead at home really shows me how "not" spiritual I am. Yes, I "party," but, it's really not so much about that; it's more of my attitude.

Since I've been here, I can see a consistent disposition in the people I meet and what it is that "separates" these types of people from the others who are "newbies" on the spiritual path. There's an unbroken dedication to want to become conscious beings, and that's becoming very apparent to me.

Being in the illumined presence of Baba constantly reveals to me my shadow self. I'm realizing that to dissipate such darkness, it requires a new way of being. *"Change your thoughts, Keith! Just change your thoughts."*

When I do get back home to Memphis, I want to make sure that I don't fall from the Grace that has lifted me up. Getting back into the music scene and grind has the power to do you in if you don't stay on top of your spiritual game. Oh, yes … I've been there, done that and bought the T-shirt. But I'm excited about the future that's going to unfold for me knowing what I'll gain from my time here in the ashram.

Today, that ole interviewitis seems to be creeping back in. A little tweak here and a little tweak there and letting that go …

done!

Isn't it funny how when we think we have reached a cool space, we are sometimes clearly shown a glimpse of an even higher dimension that's available? Yet again, we work very hard to get into a groove by processing – doing and not doing, thinking and feeling different things than we have before. While we go through these stages, we are constantly changing and ascending. We just can't see it because we are "too close" to ourselves. So, we sometimes can get frustrated in our self-evaluating myopia, believing that it all seems futile.

After one final attempt to make things go the way we want them to and when we finally say to ourselves, "Oh, the heck with it!" that's when we start to just be. It's when we release the agitation that has its claws buried within our soul that we will be in the bliss of God's reciprocating grace.

Life seems to cycle through the four stages of apply, integrate, transcend and be; one rung at a time we climb up Jacob's Ladder toward the Godhead. The realization of God can happen in a moment or can span over many lifetimes. It all depends on a person's willingness to let go of any troubles and the world. It's important to remember that, as you navigate your raft down the river of life, passion and sincerity are what'll guide you to the stream that'll push you along, all the way to the shore of a blissful forever.

I know without a doubt that I've been here on this Earth for many lifetimes and I'm bored with it. Planet Earth is beautiful, please don't get me wrong. It's just that I want to live in the lighter energies of Spirit. "But, Keith, you don't have to leave the Earth to do that," you may say. I know. I think that that's why I'm here; for Sai Baba to help me embody the Divine Principle so I can experience Heaven on Earth.

I'm still hungry! I haven't been eating any meat, so I can say that the density has definitely changed. Is this the reason? Maybe. But I think it's much deeper and broader than that. I really think this applies to all levels.

Every day without fail I've been receiving input that lifts me higher and higher. Regardless if I'm first row or last, just being present when Lord Baba walks into the hall opens Divine Doors into never-ending expansion. Yes, it's all delicious and marvelous but it's a challenge to process and contain all of this energy.

With my thoughts written and logged, I find the energy to make it to the message boards.

thought for the day
You should not, the scriptures say,
leave any remainder or balance in debts in disease,
in vengeance against enemies
in the cycle of birth and death.
Finish all down to the last.
They should not recur again.
If you offer all activities at the feet of the Lord,
And free them from any egoistic attachment,
the consequence will not bind you.
You are free, you are liberated.
You have liberation.

the other thought for the day
Love cannot bear separation from the beloved.
God, the Lord, has come down to the Earth
from Gokul to instill Divine Love in human beings.
The nature of Divine Love can be understood
only when the Divine in human form teaches
as man to man the nature of this Love.

Sai Ram, That Lady Is Me!

In Kulwant Hall for morning darshan, I notice what appears to be a father and son sitting next to me. I feel drawn to the young man, and so, I think I'll strike up a conversation with him.

"Hello, Sai Ram. What's your name?" I ask, reaching for his hand.

"My name is Arjun and this is my dad, Sasidhara," says the youngster of about eighteen.

"Hi, I'm Keith."

"What brings an American like you here to India?" he asks.

"The same thing that brings you here," I say with a big smile.

"What do you do back in America, Keith?"

"I play music full-time as a bassist and singer."

"You do? I sing, too!" he says excitedly.

"That's really neat, young man."

"After we see Lord Baba, can we go back to your room so I can hear you sing? I will sing for you, too. I love music so much; it's all I have ever wanted to do!" says Arjun, as if imaging what it's like to be me.

"Sure," I say, knowing it would make his day.

Shortly, Baba will come out to spread His Divine Love to all those here.

As always, Baba makes His way across the hall blessing all, talking to some and pointing at a few.

With Baba now on the men's side and near me, I notice a picture of Ganesh that I'd never seen before and I feel it's very important to keep looking at it.

All of sudden my mind flashes to the dream I had with Baba and Gita that I wrote about earlier. Let me share with you why I think this is relevant to me and what's happening in my life.

Ganesh, a unique combination of his elephant-like head

and a quick-moving mouse vehicle represents tremendous wisdom, intelligence, and presence of mind. Ganesh, the God of knowledge and the remover of obstacles, is also the older son of Lord Shiva. Lord Ganesha is also called Vinayak (knowledgeable) or Vighneshwer (god to remove obstacles). He is worshipped, or at least remembered, in the beginning of any auspicious performance for blessings.

He has four hands, an elephant's head and a big belly. His vehicle is a tiny mouse. In his hands he carries a rope (to carry devotees to the truth), an axe (to cut devotees' attachments), and a sweet dessert ball – laddoo (to reward devotees for spiritual activity). His fourth hand's palm is always and forever extended to bless people.

If you stop and think about it, in the natural world, elephants have the power to move anything out of their way. So, it makes sense to me that, when holding the image of Ganesh, you are stating an intention to call on the power that will remove whatever might be in your way.

Here's my interpretation of the two dreams back then and why I noticed the Ganesh picture this morning.

In the dream I had where Lord Baba asked me to wait outside all day, it didn't mean He wanted me to wait outside of my apartment. What Baba meant was, "Keith, step out of what you know as reality. The opportunity to come see Me in India is nigh." My going outside to wait for Baba on that hot day was the intention needed to make room for the manifestation of my pilgrimage. That's why Baba invited me to India. Now I get it.

Many times in dreamland I wanted to get close to Baba, but couldn't. Likewise, my ongoing attachment about always being next to Him here is what's been blocking me from having an inner view of my own self. So, in my dream with Sai Baba and Gita, the baby elephant was the birth of my own inner Ganesh and the start of the removing process that would serve me for the rest of my life.

Coincidentally, yesterday while shopping, I bought a beautiful figurine of Ganesh. When I came back into the ashram I noticed a very large statue of Him, and as many times as I've passed through those gates, how did I not see it before? This has to be one of the most powerful alignments since I've been here. What a great way to start off my morning.

With darshan now over, Baba and the lucky ones are headed into the interview room. But wait, something's amiss. There's a lady being denied access. It's my guess she's mistaken about being called as one for an interview. Ouch! I'm sure that has to hurt. My thoughts go out to her in an endless stream of love and compassion.

"Excuse me, Sai Ram. Are you still going to sing with me?" says Arjun.

"Yes … follow me."

Back in my room with Arjun and Sasidhara, the young man asks, "What would you like to sing for me, Keith?"

"I don't usually sing without music or my guitar. I really wish I had it here; let me think about it."

"You sing rock and roll?" asks Arjun.

"Yes. I sing all types of rock."

"Can you name me some songs you like to sing?" he asks.

"I like to sing Styx, Billy Joel, Bryan Adams …"

"Yes … that one! Sing me a Bryan Adams song," he says excitedly.

"What about the song, *Cuts Like a Knife*?"

"That will do just fine," he says very antsy.

Driving home this evening,
coulda sworn we had it all worked out.
You had this boy believing,
way beyond the shadow of a doubt.

On and on I go until I finish a verse and a chorus.

"Whoa … that is so cool!" exclaims Arjun, while Sasidhara applauds in the background.

"My turn … my turn!" he says, jumping up and down.

"What are you going to sing?" I ask him.

"A song by Boyzone called, *Isn't It A Wonder*."

"Go for it, dude!" I tell Arjun, as he goes into this finger-snapping, beat-boxing, Michael Jackson kind of thing.

It's a sign of the times, girl,
sad songs on the radio.
It's a sign of the times, girl,
as the leaves begin to go.
But all these signs now,
Showin' on my face.
Provin' me wrong,
Takin' its place …

"Whoa, dude, that's so cool!" I tell the starry-eyed youngster. "How old are you, Arjun?"

"I'm eighteen."

After Arjun and I talk for quite a long time about music, Sasidhara says, "Son, it's time for us to go so Mr. Keith can get back to what he needs to do."

"Okay, Father."

Shaking their hands and wishing them well, I say goodbye, somehow knowing we'll meet again one day.

Now's a perfect time to go get some inspiration from the daily thought boards.

As I make my way out of the hall and onto the ashram grounds, I hear someone say to me, "Hello, Sai Ram. How are you?"

"I'm great. How are you?" I say to the Indian lady.

"I'm good also. Can I share something with you?" she asks.

"Sure."

"You know it's not important to have an interview with Baba. If this plagues you, you must release this foolish notion," she says to me, as if knowing I've been wrestling with this.

"I know what you mean. At darshan this morning, when Baba was making His rounds, He pointed to about seven or eight people, granting them a one-on-one session. But there was this lady who was mistaken about being called and was denied access. I felt for her and sent her love."

"Sai Ram, that lady is me!" she says to me, knocking me for a loop.

"When it happened, I felt for you and your feelings about it all," I say to her.

"Then that has to be why I am here with you now; to remind you to let all the stuff I was holding onto go. It can only cause you nothing but trouble," she says, reaching to give me a hug.

"Thanks for sharing your heart and supporting me in becoming better," I say to her gratefully.

"Thank you, too, Sai Ram," she says, while walking away with a smile.

This alignment and realization thing is hitting me so hard that I have to sit down for a bit before I proceed to get some food and make my way to afternoon darshan.

On the concrete slab and munching on the usual cheese crackers, I'm waiting to see Lord Baba. But, being late and literally the last one to sit down, it's not likely that I'll be close to Him because I didn't make darshan my highest priority.

"Line 9, please stand up and go to the hall," says the man with the clipboard.

"Oh, my God ... that's my line ... we are first!"

I spring up from my position with delight, knowing that I'll again be up front and close to the Love who inspires millions of people to become Divine with Him. *"I think I'm starting to get the hang of this letting go of attachments thing."*

Darshan and bhajans just finished and I'm walking toward

the daily thought boards. Today's blessing was typical: Baba greeted people, healed some, took their letters and created some things here and there. But, while singing bhajans, I fell so far inside of myself that I had an amazing vision of Krishna. It was very clear; almost to the point of becoming an apparition.

thought for the day
In ancient times,
the sages performed rigorous penance in the forest
living among wild animals.
With no weapons in the hands,
they relied on the spirit of Love to protect them.
They performed their penance
with Love for all beings.
Their Love transformed even the wild animals
which live at peace with the sages.
Love transformed even tigers into friendly beast.

the other thought for the day
There is no need to establish
a new religion or a new institution.
The world needs only
men and women of good qualities.

The Return of Christ

"Some believe that Jesus will arrive on a white horse; that His coming will be signaled by the parting of clouds, heralded by the trumpeting of angels. Others believe that Christ will be manifested only in souls who make themselves available. Which is correct?"

Here is the most accurate way to view the return of Christ: it is not an either/or situation. It would be more correct to say that both these scenarios are facets of the truth.

Yes, the white horse is true, but not in the way many imagine. That prophecy refers to the comet Hale-Bopp that hurtled through space in the 98th year of the last century. The purpose of its trajectory was to give the world an advance sign of the return of the One you have known as Jesus.

"When will He return?"

Would you believe Me if I told you that He is already on Earth?

"Right now?"

Yes, He arrived as a child in July of 2000. The white-tailed comet was the metaphorical horse upon which He arrived.

"You mean …"

Yes, Keith, I mean that the dream you had eighteen years ago *was* real – Jesus has been born again as one of you. Time and again over the past few years, I have offered you validation of this, especially when you were in India. Why is the truth so difficult for you to believe and accept?

"I don't think I can answer Your question right now."

Because of what you think others might say about you when this book enters the public's field of awareness?

"Yes, I'm sure that's a major part of it."

I recognize your reservations, but if you have concerns about people's "How dare you!" attitude, then the best way to respond to them is with understanding and love.

"It doesn't seem to matter how many times You tell me, I still worry that this 'Jesus is born again' idea is something I've concocted in my head. Surely You can see how nervous I am about this."

What is it you are trying to say?

"I want to do the 'right' thing!"

Yes, I know, and your intention to do just that is why I am telling you this.

"Please tell me again exactly what You would like me to do."

Your job is to inform others about Jesus' return as a person. I admit, it will not be an easy task because, as we just spoke of, many have expectations that He will show up in one particular way or another.

"Will You tell me where He was born this time?"

Patience, Dear One. I shall not be revealing that to you just yet. Right now, it is enough for you to know that His human presence will be integral to Divine energies becoming more firmly anchored.

"Why is He hidden from the public's awareness?"

There are two reasons. The first is so that He can avoid distractions and unwanted attention as He prepares for His actual appearance.

The second is because He is not yet ready, nor are you. If He goes public too soon, many will not believe their eyes nor take well to the idea that He has come. Until there has been enough of a shift in clarity and understanding, His entrance will serve no purpose.

You see, there is an order to the Divine Will that must play out in sequence. At the right time, He will set out to help humanity transcend its collective ego by showing you the difference between reality (living in Love) and non-reality (living in fear). Thus will the pandemic of fear and greed come to an end.

As for Christ manifesting in individuals, well, right now,

there are many such active souls on Earth, yourself included. Some of you will not only pave the way for the Teacher whose sole/Soul purpose is to give of Himself as He did before, but you will also deflect any who would try to thwart His mission.

"What do You mean? He is Jesus the Christ, so doesn't He have enough power to protect Himself from any adversaries?"

Oh, you mean the same power He had the last time – when He was crucified?

"I see Your point."

As I said, you each have your part to play.

"God, I pray that I can be in His inner circle, be there with Him and for Him to help in any way I can!"

Beloved, you are already in His inner circle and you are being a great help by writing the words you are writing about Him. But He is not done with you yet.

"What do You mean?"

A few years hence, He will come to you again and give you instructions about further work you are to do.

"But what ..."

I know your mind must be racing, Keith, but for now, just rest it. In time, all your questions will be cleared up.

"Phew! I'll try."

Now that the birth has happened, do not be surprised if you wake up one morning and find that something inside you just feels different. And do not be surprised if the whole world feels the same way, even though their reactions may not be the same as yours. Many will choose to talk about the changes they are feeling; many more will purposely deny and ignore them. But, since you are aligning yourself, you will know intuitively what is soon to transpire.

"And what will that be?"

Jesus announcing His presence in the world.

"Doesn't Scripture state that no one except God in Heaven is supposed to know of His return and that it will come like a thief in the night?"

Yes, it is true that I am the only One who knows, but now I am telling you. And even though people will learn this from your work, when He does show up, you can bet that some will still cry "false prophet" or say that Satan has disguised himself as the Holy Light mentioned in Scripture. (2 Corinthians 11:13–15) You can bet the news of His coming will spark much debate. What the other part of the passage means is that if one does not develop the Christ within themselves – because they are too busy looking outward and/or skyward – then Christ will pass them by like a thief in the night. The only way for anyone to truly believe that He is who He says He is, is to develop the ability to recognize Truth within themselves.

I will tell you how to recognize not only Jesus, but any true teacher of God:

1) If the teacher teaches unconditional love.

2) If the teacher does not claim to be god over you, but rather, helps you to see that you are his/her equal *in* God.

Dear One, you have mentioned several times how concerned you are with what you are receiving and writing.

Let Me assure you that the Source is a Pure One. My concern is about what you will do with it. Will you close this manuscript now, never to write in it again, or do you want to continue?

"I'm really loving what I'm learning. Keep it coming!"

Good, because I have more to share with you.

Jesus, like you, was born to natural parents. The purpose of His return to Earth as a human is so that you can all see the Christ Light in yourselves once again. And as you come to see His humanity, you will also see your own divinity.

"Will He begin to teach as a child or will He wait until He is older?"

He will begin very early by exemplifying the childlike qualities of purity, innocence, acceptance and wonderment. His simple ways will serve as a counterpoint to the arrogance of adults and show them how, by living their lives the way they have, their egos have been allowed to take root, grow and bring about the chaos of today's world.

Yes, Jesus will begin to actively teach those around Him, sharing His genuine, pure disposition for all to see (the same as every child's before he/she is tainted with dogma, rules and ideas of separation).

When He makes Himself known, many will be afraid. But let Me make it clear that it is not the Child they will fear. What will cause them to be afraid will be their refusal to let go of their long-held beliefs.

Insofar as enlightenment is concerned, ignorance is not bliss. All ignorance does is invite fear. The most powerful tool to eliminate fear is a mind open to receiving information. This is why I come: to enlighten everyone so that you will not be left trembling in the dark.

Let Me expound further on the other Christs that are active now. They are everywhere imaginable! One could be living next door to you; one could be standing behind you in the checkout line; one could be your newspaper boy or your bank teller. All, like you, are committed to becoming conscious. They are working on themselves to prepare for change, all the while promulgating the changes they are on Earth to bring about. They see themselves as the crew of the Messiah-ship, the ones who will lead everyone to the Mothership.

Some of these Christ apprentices – the Children of Light – are born with special abilities and can do things beyond what some may be willing to believe or accept. Some are living amongst you and more will come, bringing with them Divine Vision and Divine Power.

For example, there are children living in South America who

display phenomenal feats of telekinesis, who can bend spoons and move objects without touching them. If you ever come in contact with any of these children, look into their eyes and you will see the Light of Spirit.

These children (who are beginning to gather together) are different from most, for they are born with an intact awareness. They know where they have been, they know who they are and they know the purpose of their mission.

Furthermore, unlike most adults who have only two active DNA strands, these children have between eight and twelve active strands of DNA. It is in these multiple active strands that the Children of Light store Divine information and power they can use at will. And, since their will is unified with that of the Divine Will, they act accordingly.

"So You're telling me I only have two strands? What's up with that?"

Nothing personal, Keith, just a fail-safe means to keep everyone from abusing everyone else. There are far too many people that would use such power to control, so I only bestow it on those who are conscious of My plan.

"I see what You mean. I can't tell You how many times I hear people say, 'Kids nowadays are disturbed, nothing but rebellious out-of-control punks that must be restrained.'"

Let Me ask you, does attempting to control them ever work?

"Hardly ever."

How right you are! Even when adults attempt to exercise control, kids still express themselves in the very behaviors that adults are trying to discourage. I give children freedom of expression and adults try to take it away – go figure!

Oh, I agree, kids *are* rebellious and it is in their very nature to oppose anyone who tries to extinguish their spirit's light. The way they dress, many have a problem with. The way they look, many have a problem with. The way they act, many have a problem with. What they think they stand for, many have a problem with. Whatever they do that differs from the norm, many have a problem with. Indeed, who they are, many have a problem with.

"No wonder they rebel!"

But all these problems really begin with the ones who regard kids' behavior as a problem. You see, it is no big deal to Me if kids get tattoos or pierce every body part. What "concerns" Me is those who would try to pierce children's hearts with the daggers of their own egos!

The intent of every adult should be to never hurt children, but rather to help them reach their fullest potential to inspire change. When you find it within yourselves to be permissive, grateful and humble around them, it will help all of you to acknowledge who you once were and, in essence, still are, and why I bestow power upon the Children of Light and not adults.

Yes, you as adults must acknowledge children as people. Learn what they have to offer you. Sit and talk with them for a while and they will enlighten you with the simple wisdom that can only be coming from deep within.

Children should not be thought of as delinquents! Believe it or not, they have the vision to improve your world – if only you will let them. All they ask is the right of Self-expression. But the truth is, they need not ask. You see, I have already given them *My* permission!

"Earlier, You said that special children are gathering. How many are there?"

Interesting you should ask. They number fewer than you might imagine and they do not behave that differently from the way you did in your adolescence.

The Children of Light prefer to join up with "normal" kids and run as a pack. That way, they can live amongst you, yet remain hidden from the "wolves" until the time is right.

"So You're saying that the kids they run with have a purpose as well."

Yes, and together they form the mission of the Children of Light.

"Do these Children of Light live only in South America?"

Not necessarily, but no matter where they are, those imbued with Spirit's power are lying low until the time is right. When that time comes, they will emerge and lead the way to change. What do you think people will do then?

"I think many will boycott anything they have to offer."

Right you are. Once again, what they say and do, many will have a problem with! But try to thwart it (though some might), an awareness will happen and eventually people will understand.

"This may be off the subject, but I want to tell You how sad I am that we adults have managed to screw up the world so badly."

Ah, but that *is* indeed the subject, Beloved, and that will change!

"When?"

When you choose to follow the guidance of a special Child. I bet you never thought that a child would be the one to set you on your spiritual path.

"Oh, Jesus, of course! It's all beginning to make sense to me now. Based on what I've learned, it would take a child to save us from ourselves!"

Together, these Children will teach Self-expression.
Together, these Children will teach Peace.
Together, these Children will teach Love.
And together, these Children will teach Unity – God.

PREPARE FOR THE RETURN OF THE CHRIST!

Oh, My God!

Waking up and rubbing my eyes, I'm late getting down to the concrete slab again, and if I don't get my butt moving, my chances to be next to Sai Baba might dwindle. Even though I mentioned earlier that the lines are called randomly, I still like to do whatever I can to show my intention for getting a sweet spot.

Flying out of the door, I forgot to take with me the jade japamala I bought the other day in the hopes Baba would bless it. *"I have to go back and get it!"*

Heading back to Kulwant Hall, I feel just how cold it can be in the early morning hours. "Stay centered by breathing, Keith. It will pass," I hear from within.

I have the feeling there's more carrying over from yesterday that will come into view today. One thing on my mind is how, ever since I've been here, I've been asking Baba to visit me in a dream.

Sitting and waiting for just over an hour, I'm finally in the hall on the second row. Looking around, I notice the gentleman next to me with a book titled *Sathya Sai Baba and Jesus Christ.* Seems interesting. I'll have to buy that book at the Sai Bookstore later.

After the morning rituals, Baba comes through the gate on the women's side in all His Glory doing what He always does. When He gets to the men's side, He immediately comes in my direction. *"Why do I that feel something very significant is about to occur?"* Here He comes ... here He comes ... here He is! My hand immediately goes up holding the jade prayer bead for Him to bless. Looking at me strangely, He skips right over me. I can't believe He just did that! Why? All He had to do was bless the bead after He blessed those around me. I don't get it.

Now that Baba has finished morning darshan, I'm going back

to my room to get a little more sleep. I wonder if there's any reason for my sleep pattern being so unusual. Is it because my body is still adjusting from jet lag? I don't know.

I look out the window from my bed and see that the ashram is being remodeled. *"Say what?"* Now, I can't sleep! There's too much going through my mind like, why did it take me all this time to notice they are renovating the ashram? Why hadn't I noticed it before? Out of all the books I've read about Baba and His Leelas (Divine Sport), many of them say that one should always pay close attention to their surroundings, especially when in the ashram.

The fact that this redoing of the ashram is taking place could be telling the group that's here now they are also being transformed and made anew. This is definitely the case for me. If there are seasons for everything, then it makes perfect sense this would be the manifestation of such a time. Equally, I'd guess there would be periods when groups come just for support and not a new birth such as what could be happening with this group.

It's amazing the magic that happens when one is open to see how things work on all levels; as above, so below. Wide awake, I think I'll go hang in the courtyard to do some meditation and talk with people until the afternoon darshan.

On my way to the courtyard, I get the feeling that I should step out of the ashram gates for some reason. Why? I don't know; it has to be something important.

Stepping into the street I feel drawn to a little shop.

"Can I help you, sir?" says an Indian man with thick glasses.

"You sure can," I reply.

"What is it that you would like me to get for you?" he asks.

"What is it you think I need?" I say to him, trusting that he has it.

"Here you go! Take this beautiful japamala for your prayers to Baba."

"Yes. That's exactly what I want," I reply, as I reach for my wallet to pay him, and then walk away.

What a beautiful prayer bead. It's clear with an orange tassel like the color Sai Baba wears.

On my way to the courtyard to say prayers on my new japamala, I find that I'm getting very sleepy again. But my sleepiness seems kind of strange. I mean, at home in Memphis, I'd take a nap every day, but not until about three o'clock or so. I haven't napped since I've been here. And, what's odd is that this drowsiness feels like I've taken a nighttime cold medicine.

"Oh, my God!"

I just got up from my nap with a most amazing experience to tell. During my sleep, I was brought to a state of complete consciousness by Baba. Why now?

In the experience, a small group of people, including myself, were sitting in the bleachers of a gymnasium, while Sai Baba was standing in the middle of the court. After getting my wits about me, Baba turned His hand and created a gold chest. It was sacred, old and looked like the Ark of the Covenant. It had carvings, scripture and intricate detail all over it.

Someone reached to touch it and I advised him not to do that.

"Why not?" he asked.

"Because this chest looks to be more special than anything we've ever seen. There's no telling what kind of effect it can have on you, us and its Divine Purpose," I told him.

Just then, Sai Baba chimed in to say, "It's for us to touch together. Everyone step forward, grab the cover, hold it tight and we will lift it on my mark." At this point, I'm so excited knowing that whatever's inside is going to be full of magic.

"Ready, here we go ... LIFT!" said Baba. After the beautiful cover was off and put to the side, I began to focus on what was there on the floor. It was a solid-gold, nativity-type scene. Just when my eyes became fixed on the simplicity of its design, Baba said to the group, "Look! What do you see?"

In unison, we said, "We see a throne, two goats and a crib."

"What do you think these things mean?" asks Baba. No one said a word. At this point, He looks directly to me saying, "Keith, I am going to tell you something you already know. You have known this for a while – since your birth. These figurines of a throne, two goats and a crib represent the return of Christ. Again, you are being told that Jesus, the man who achieved Christ Consciousness 2,000 years ago, will be born again on Earth in five months."

After a quick blackout, the experience then went to a Burger King Restaurant in South Louisiana, where a pickup truck carrying Lord Baba in the back pulled up. Everyone in the parking lot knew He was coming and wanted Him to help them find something they'd lost. My impression was they lost water.

Baba stepped out of the truck, dug into a pocket from His robe and threw a handful of gold coins on the ground. Everyone immediately dropped to their knees hoping to grab one. Baba then said, "People, stand up and gain from Me what you have lost!" That's when I woke up crying profusely to tell you of this prophetic message Baba just imparted to me about Jesus.

After weeping for about thirty minutes, I find myself starting to get very angry with God. Let me explain.

Ever since I was a little boy, I always knew that Jesus would come back in my lifetime. Before I started writing *The Divine Principle*, thoughts of His return began to fall into my mind as if to tell me to pay attention because somehow I was going to be involved with it.

A few years passed and I found myself beginning to write a chapter titled, "The Return of Christ." I wrote this segment with no expectation of ever including it in the book, but to just vent out fanciful ideas that seemed to be clogging my head.

After a while, the chapter started taking shape and was very juicy as far as the punch, clarity and inspiration it seemed to have. I thought to myself, *"This is a good chapter! Too bad because,*

I can't use it."

Lo' and behold, that night after falling asleep, I was visited by two angels. They spoke as one voice in each ear telling me, "Keith, keep the chapter. There is more that will come for you to insert. We have told you ever since you were a child that the one you know as Jesus would return. Log what we are telling you and leave the rest to us." So, I accepted their message and began to work on the chapter with absolute conviction of the Lord's return and included it in my book.

Two years go by and I find myself in Baba's ashram with my face buried in my hands. I'm crying from my soul because Baba told me in a dream that Jesus will be born again in five months and I don't know what I'm supposed to do about it. Underneath all of that, I feel very angry. Why? Because after the two angels told me to write and publish that chapter, which I did, it now all seems like a big game, which I don't want to play anymore. Who in the world would want to toy with Christian faith followers' love for their Lord with false information? Surely, not me!

To let you know how angry I feel, I'm cursing at God (Baba) with words sailors won't even use.

A few minutes have gone by and I'm now feeling better about this. I've vented out all of my frustration and my concerns have been heard.

Calming down, I drift into a light meditation.

"Okay, Baba. I need your attention! This has come up yet again. If my prophetic dream with You was real and You told me this because I'm somehow supposed to play whatever role in the unfoldment, I'll definitely need something from You right here and now. I need to know the TRUTH!" I pray on my new japamala, knowing I have to be very clear about what I say.

"I need to know if what I've heard about Jesus' return since I was a child, what the angels have told me and now what You are telling me is to be valid as I understand it. Are You telling me that this is not a metaphor and that Jesus Christ is literally coming back to this planet in five months – and You want me to tell people about it? If this is the Absolute Truth, then show me that You heard me!"

I continue to pray "… Baba, what I want to know is, is what I've just experienced about Lord Jesus' return valid? Is it valid? Is it valid?" Over and over with great fervor I ask, "Is it valid?"

After saying this prayer for hours, I'm now sitting on the concrete waiting area and I'm determined to keep it up until Baba gives us His darshan.

"Line 3, stand up and make your way into the hall," says the man with the clipboard. *"Yes … first row!"* I shoot to my feet and march into the hall for only God knows what, while I continue to roll my new prayer bead around in my hand.

Sitting in a first-row spot, I fall into meditation; over and over I continue my prayer: "Baba, is it valid?"

About an hour later, something inside tells me that my prayer is complete. When I open my eyes, I'm startled by a Seva Dal staring at me. I mean, he's right in front of my face mirroring me in lotus position. He's so close that, if he was any closer, his knees would be touching mine.

"Keith, My son, look down," whispers a voice. BANG! – a miracle happens as my heart bursts wide open. I'm looking at the attendant's ID badge and it says … yes, you guessed it, "Valid 2000." There's also a pen in his shirt pocket with an image of Sai Baba waving as if to say, "Yes, it's me doing all of this and it's valid, Keith."

"Sai Ram, why is your ID badge turned around backwards?" I ask the man in a shaky voice.

"It happens once in a while," he says, while turning it the right way. BANG! – another miracle. The front of his badge says: He lives at #5 Cross Street which points to the event happening in five months as Baba said and today is the fifth. Cross Street relates to Jesus obviously. The Seva Dal's first name is Yana, and that happens to be a spiritual name I've been going by for quite some time.

"What does that mean on the back side of your ID badge?" I ask, pointing to it.

Leaning into me as if to give me a message from Lord Baba he whispers, "That means it's valid."

"Oh, my God!" I'm catapulted into Heaven and feeling the most amazing bliss because of what just occurred.

With Baba in the hall on the women's side and working His way over to the men's, I'm so excited that I don't know what to think or do.

Now Baba is walking toward me and I know this is my moment. "Is it valid?" I pray a few more times, or, at least until He gets as close as I know He's going to.

Although Baba is near, He still hasn't noticed me. He seems to be busy with someone across the aisle and facing the other way. But, something inside is telling me that this is the moment to act. So, I take a deep breath, put one hand over my heart, raise up my prayer bead with the other and pray. "Baba?" I ask. "You with all my love and responsibility for such a prophecy – Is it valid?" Suddenly, Sai Baba stops what He is doing, turns around and walks straight over to me, as my heart pounds in my chest. Blessing my japamala, Sai Baba touches my hand and looks right into my eyes. BANG! – Yet another miracle. "That's why I skipped over you this morning with the jade bead, Keith. I set you up to give you something of great magnitude. Enjoy the ride, My Son!" I hear Him say telepathically, as I'm pulled into the universe, see Truth of Baba and the truth of the prophecy given to me. Oh, Sweet Lord! I even see me as the personality self looking through His eyes. With my consciousness and heart now expanded, I fall very deep within, experience the birth of Creation and become a sobbing mess of bliss.

The glimpse Sai Baba has just given me is so powerful and overwhelming that I have to leave the hall; I don't want to be a distraction to everyone else. I'll need to gain some sort of composure before I try to walk.

Leaving Kulwant Hall, I'm doing whatever I can to stay in the bliss of validation energy and just appreciate my life. Maybe the thought for the day will expound on all that has just transpired.

thought for the day
If I pin a badge on your apparel,
you will unpin it soon.
When it is taken off the shirt,
you will feel relieved that you have been released from the
obligation to love and serve.
You will only play a temporary role in the drama
doubting the badge off and on.
Wear the invisible badge of a volunteer of God
at all hours and in all places.
Let all the days of living be a contiguous offering
of love as an oil lamp exhaust itself
in illuminating the surroundings.
Bend the body, mend the senses and the mind,
that is the process of obtaining the status
of the children of immortality which
the Upanishads have reserved for man.

the other thought for the day
Everything is born out of pure love.
All joy is derived from an alloyed love.
So are truth, sacrifice, peace and forbearance.
If love is lacking, there can be no contentment.
This the path of Sai and the word of truth.

Going Home

I'm up and at 'em, packing my stuff to head home. As much as I can't wait to see my girlfriend, friends, family and bandmates, equally, I don't want to leave this lovely place. But, there's a season for everything, and right now, it's going home.

Soon, I'll go to my final darshan to thank Baba and ask Him for His blessings to be with me throughout my life.

On my way to Kulwant Hall, I stop by the courtyard to admire its beauty one last time. Upon arriving, I find a lady who looks as if she is doing the same thing.

"Excuse me, Sai Ram. How are you this morning?" I ask.

"Good morning, Sai Ram. I am filled with bliss looking at the Sun as it shines Its love over this beautiful ashram," she replies.

"My thoughts exactly," I say with a smile.

"Today is my last day here with Sai Baba. What about you?" she asks.

"Same as you," I say with a chuckle.

"Can I share something that happened to me yesterday?" asks the lady.

"I'd like nothing more," knowing that whatever it is, it was going to be frickin' magical.

"Yesterday, I had the blessed opportunity to go into the interview room after darshan to be with Lord Baba. When the session was over, I approached some of the people in there to ask them about what they had experienced, but not everyone spoke the same language. This left me very puzzled because we all understood what Baba was saying when He was saying it. The miracle of that moment is still with me and creating the space for me to share the bliss that I feel now with you. It is a great day to be alive, isn't it?" says the beautiful soul.

"To hear your story makes it so," I say with tears in my eyes.

"Thank you very much for the chat and our brief time together, Sai Ram, but now I must get down to Kulwant Hall for darshan before I head back to the States."

"I must do exactly the same, and thank you!"

Sitting on the fourth row in Kulwant Hall for my last darshan, I have an endless reverence and respect for the time I've spent here with God in human form. As I look around with such love for this ashram, the people in it and what this abode stands for, my heart is filled with beauty and joy. It feels like today, in this moment, that my trip here is now being solidified within me.

As you might imagine, the parade, the bell ringing, the twenty-one "Aum" mantra and Baba's presence in the hall this morning are going to be very different for me than all the days before. I have no doubt that the humility I fall into will be sacred.

If this passage is being treated as a poem, there needs to be lines before and after it.

Here comes the parade down the street,
and it's truly a celebration of Love.
I rejoice in it.
There goes the bell, filling all ears and hearts,
asking God to awaken and walk on the Earth.
I am ready to receive.
There goes the twenty-one "Aum" mantra.
I affirm that I am here and present.
And, there's Sai Baba coming through the gate.
I am humbled, grateful, in love
and blessed beyond imagination.

There isn't much to tell about darshan, or rather, not much that I remember. It all seems foggy, as if it were a dream – a beautiful dream.

When I saw Sai Baba a moment ago, it was like I fell into a

warm and nurturing cocoon. And, I absolutely know that I'm not supposed to stay here one more day. I'm supposed to get on that plane, go home and begin to spread all of the love and grace I've felt here.

This is my final trip to a thought board, then I'll be heading back to Memphis.

thought for the day

It is to transform man's nature from
the animal to the human
that love has been serving as a powerful force.
The hearts of men, in the olden days,
were soft and loving.
Although love is inherently soft and compassionate,
in certain situations it assumes a stern form.
This is because even out of love,
one has sometimes to use punishment.
The harsh words and punishment
are associated with love.
When it rains, it is a downpour of drops of water.
But sometimes
the rain is accompanied by hailstorms.
The hailstorms are hard
but they are only water in condensed form.
Likewise, softness or punishment
are different expressions of love.

I'm in a taxi with Ana's aunt, Rasa, for the long trek back to Bangalore and I'm already missing the ashram and Baba.

Rasa is an illumined, grandmother-type of lady, but definitely not slow in the mind nor on her feet. What's magical is that, even though we don't speak the same language, we still understand each other.

In her best attempt, Rasa is telling me the story of how Sai

Baba manifested a silver ring, embossed with a gold bust of Himself, that snuggly fit on her finger.

"Can I have it?" I ask with a huge smile on my face.

"No!" she says, clutching the ring and laughing.

"Well, that was very clear."

Back and forth we are telling amazing stories using simple words, lots of hand gestures and our telepathic will about how Sri Sathya Sai Baba has forever changed our lives.

All Is Well

I just got to the Airport in Bangalore and found out from the lady behind the desk that I'm not allowed to fly into Mumbai. I had no idea that I was supposed to contact them 72 hours in advance to secure my flight. This isn't a good thing! I'm begging her with a juicy story but she's not budging.

I quickly pray to Baba, "I need your help!"

"Is there a problem here?" asks a lady that walked out of a secured door from the right and over to us.

"This young man did not make contact with the airline 72 hours before his flight. And so, I told him that he could not board," she says.

"That is our policy, Mr. ...? ... Mr. Blanchard," says the manager, looking at my passport and then back at me.

After scanning me up and down to make sure nothing was amiss, she gave her approval, "Let him go."

"Oh, thank you ... Om Sai Ram!" I say with delight.

And, as her eyes light up with a smile, I take off as fast I can toward the plane that I almost missed.

Fastening my seatbelt, there seems to be a fear of flying creeping in and I don't know why. I generally have no problem when it comes to flying, but right now, this really has its claws in me.

"Attention, passengers, please prepare yourselves for our departure from Bangalore to North India," says the captain over the PA system.

"Hi. My name is Keith," I say very chipper to a man next to me, trying to divert my attention from the nagging fear.

"My name is Dan," he replies, not so chipper back.

"Do you fly often, Dan?" I went on to distract my focus from the takeoff.

"No," he says.

"When is the last time you flew?" I ask.

"Keith, the last time I flew I was in a horrible plane crash and everyone died but me," he tells me with a sad and scared look on his face.

"Oh, my God!" thinking to myself.

"I'm so sorry to have bothered you," I say to the timid fellow.

"No worries. I'm just very tired and need some rest, that's all."

"Nice to meet you, brother, and be well," I say, as he closes his eyes and leans into a pillow.

"That was freaky! Now, what am I supposed to do with this fear of my mortality?"

Oh, wow! There's a major alignment here. I felt this coming on way before I boarded the plane. Maybe that fear was not mine after all. Maybe it was Dan's. I must have been incredibly empathic, taking on what he was feeling. I wonder if this is something I'll be developing in life; the ability to feel others' feelings.

Realizing this, my fear has dissipated as if it never happened. Maybe I should start paying more attention to this kind of experience in my future.

Relaxed and settling back in my seat, I begin to run through my mind all the miracles that have transpired in the last two weeks. What an amazing, life-changing journey to India this has been. There's so much inside of me that I can't begin to process any of this right now. So, I'll just close my eyes and think about the people back home that I love until I doze off.

Tonight I'll be staying at a Four Seasons Hotel in Mumbai. My buddy pass has limitations, and when it comes to a full plane, revenue passengers come first, so I'll have to wait for the next flight. I'm here, so I might as well take advantage of this opportunity and see the city.

The young man who found me my room suggested I visit the Krishna Temple which will make my layover worthwhile. The two things he has done for me so far are right on the money, but the tip he's asking for is not. I like this guy, so what the heck; I grant him his wish.

Walking into my room for the night, I see that it's very nice. For just 75 bucks I have a luxury suite that overlooks the Arabian Sea. This trip keeps getting better and better, even on my way home. I love it!

On both of my trips to and from the ashram, it's evident that I was and I am still being watched over and guided by strangers. Leaving me with the secure feeling that all is well, I dive into the bed for a good night's rest in the cool air-conditioning.

The Layover

"Mr. Keith Blanchard?" I hear with an Indian accent and a soft knock on the door. "Are you ready to go to the Temple? I have your rickshaw ready and waiting for you downstairs," says the gentleman who found me my room.

"Give me fifteen minutes and I'll be right down."

I slept in this morning because the bed was so comfortable and the temperature in the room was just perfect. Besides, I have nothing to do today except go to the Krishna Temple before I head back home.

"Hello, Mr. Blanchard," says the helper, as I walk up to him.

"Please remind me. What's your name?"

"Suraj. My name is Suraj."

"Are you ready now?" he asks, bobbling his head.

"I am."

"Climb in."

This is my first rickshaw ride and I'm really digging it. Now, I get to see just what it's like to scoot around Mumbai, dodging all the chaos.

As soon as we get rolling, car horns blast at us because of our weaving in and out of traffic.

"Mr. Keith, don't worry. Be happy!" says Suraj, looking over his shoulder, knowing that my fingers are embedded into the back of his seat.

"I trust you, Suraj."

"Good!" as he full throttles toward town.

Pulling up to the Temple, Suraj says, "I will be here waiting when you are finished with the tour."

"How long will that take?" I ask.

"About an hour. No worries, I have some things I can do while you are in there," he replies.

"I will see you in about an hour then," as I watch him take off in his rickshaw.

Arriving at the Temple and looking around, I'm amazed by the energy. I see big, beautiful pictures of Krishna, Rama and many other Hindu deities don the walls. As in Sai Baba's ashram, mostly everyone here is wearing white Punjabis. The wearing of white clothing is said to allow one's aura to be more visible, making for better communication and synergy between all the devotees.

"Sir? Come this way. Stand here and move with the line," says an elderly man with few teeth and nerdy glasses.

"Thank you!" I say with appreciation.

Moving around the Temple with the other tourists, I'm being shown places where rituals are practiced. The guide who is speaking in a soft voice is telling us about Its history and of the Masters who reside/d here throughout time.

I must say, though the customs are different here to that in Sai Baba's ashram, it doesn't seem to matter what deity is being revered; it all feels the same to me, whether I was going to a seminary to be a priest, on Baba's ashram or here in this place.

I think an important awakening that one could have happen is when one comes to know that God actively dwells within all who love, regardless of the belief or religion.

My tour of the Krishna Temple is over and I'm sitting outside waiting for Suraj to pick me up. I open up a book from my bag to find this passage by Sai Baba:

"The basic message is eternal. It was taught by Christ, Buddha, Krishna, Mohammed and others. The message is essentially as Jesus gave on the Sermon on the Mount, and stresses the unity of all creation; the Fatherhood of God and the Brotherhood of man.

There is only one caste; the caste of humanity.
There is only one religion; the religion of love.
There is only one language; the language of the heart.

There is only one God, and He is omnipresent."

After reading this excerpt into my tape recorder, my helper pulls up next to me in his rickshaw.

"Sai Ram, how did you like your visit?"

"It was beautiful and full of meaning," I reply.

"Yes. I can tell you liked it very much."

"Here we are, Mr. Blanchard," as we arrive at the hotel.

"Thank you very much!" I tell him.

"But, Sai Ram ... are you going to tip me? I've been a big help to you, yes?"

"Yes, you have. But, don't you remember that big tip I gave you yesterday?"

"Oh, of course I do." Then off he jets to find someone else to assist.

Before I head toward the airport, I think I'll go to my room to browse through the books I bought in the ashram. Speaking of books, there are two big boxes of them that will travel six months by ship to be delivered to my apartment in Memphis. The shipment contains the entire thirty-volume set of the *Sathya Sai Speaks* series. These books were created over the years from Baba's discourses; scribed and fashioned around the teachings that Baba has given throughout His life.

"What's this?" reaching for a book from my bag titled *Sathya Sai Baba and Jesus Christ: A Gospel for the Golden Age*. It seems to parallel the life of Christ and Sai Baba. Hmmm? This must be the book I was going to get that I mentioned in the chapter, "Oh, My God!", but I don't remember ever buying it. Could it be that someone is toying with me again? Eh, doesn't matter, it sounds awesome. I think I'll read through it until it's time for me to leave.

"Whoa!" What I'm reading right now is so relevant to what Baba said about Jesus coming back that the excerpt I'm inserting here will perfectly describe what happened to me and how my

heart burst open when Baba looked into my eyes.

A Vision of God

"He walked by me every day the one they call the Christ. He blessed some, ignored others, I don't know why.

I wanted to meet His eyes to see the face of God, but He did not see me. He saw everyone else, not me. Why not me?

Then one day, one wonderful day, He stood close by. I gazed into His face, and for a moment, His eyes met mine. In those eyes was Infinity more profound than space, more potent than the sun, all-knowing, all-seeing.

Like Adam, I was naked before Him. He saw me, what I am, what I could be, what I have attained and where I have failed. He saw my past, my present and my future. He saw all my sins and blemishes, my ego and my pride.

He saw also what I can be in Him if only I would surrender to Him, to give up my faults and errors, my ego and my pride.

His eyes held compassion for sorrows I bring upon myself. His eyes held love for me despite who I am. His eyes held the universe and all of us in it. In His eyes I recognized my God, my Creator, my Master.

I saw also myself reflected as the Image of God. I felt my soul being drawn into His eyes as if in a moment I could be one with Him, not the petty self anymore, but a new creature in whom God shines forth. Then His eyes looked away and my life was forever changed.

For one eternal, precious moment I saw Divinity. I saw God and He saw me. His eyes turned away, but He still sees me."

As I said, what you've just read is exactly how I felt during that "Jesus being born" experience in Kulwant Hall with Sai Baba. I really hope you are able to get at least a glimpse of what I'm talking about.

I'm feeling an inner prompting to insert this message from

Baba that I found a while back:

"Embodiments of the Divine Atma:

By forgetting his own true nature and being carried away by the pleasures of the external world which are both fleeting and superficial and by trying to secure and experience such material pleasures, man fritters away his life and fritters away his time.

Is man able to secure peace by experiencing and obtaining these material pleasures? No! At the end of life he is dissatisfied and discontented.

Man has become ignorant of the permanent being within him which is truth itself and formless. He is reducing himself to the state of an animal and becomes demonic in the process. Ultimately, man comes to the end of his life without a sense of fulfillment because he is not able to understand the purpose of it and his own true nature.

What is the cause for this? He neglects the Supreme code of conduct laid down before him; the code of dharma, right action, that he has to follow. Man has forgotten that dharma, the Divine Order, is at the base of everything, and that this dharma is most important for his own character.

The perfection of character by discrimination is the royal path for any human being. It is the very purpose, aim and goal of one's life. The respect, honor and dignity of the human race depends upon the character that is exhibited. Without it, the race itself would come to ruin. The improvement of character can indeed be called the hallmark of a human being. Only when morality and ethics range high in the set of values, can an individual realize the Divine Atma within.

The name for dharma, the Divine Order, is Love. Nobody can describe love or how valuable it is. The various ideas about love do not designate True Love, which has no streak of selfishness and never changes. Everything that is sacred and sanctified can be found in this True Love. If it is furthered and nourished, that type of love will always increase and never decrease.

There is no reason for this love. That True Love is without reason, without selfishness and never waivers or changes, but is forever full and total. That is the Love of God. The ordinary love exhibited by human beings has a certain reason behind it. It has a note of selfishness in it and it changes with the passage of time. Therefore, it is impossible for men who feel this human love to understand the Love of God. What I wish to convey to you is that the love of a human being is totally different from the Love of God.

As I said earlier, your love is motivated by selfishness. It depends upon some reason and is temporary. My Love is selfless with no reason and has no end. Through My Love I am fostering and nourishing your love. Your love is thus nourished by this Supreme Love. So you should see to it that you live this Supreme Love and that you do not harm or injure any being, as I would not harm or injure anyone. One should realize the Divinity of God and the Love of God and live in Love with the hope you will be a model of this Love to the world.

Start the day with Love. Spend the day with Love. End the day with Love. This is the way to God."

Home Sweet Home

I'm now back home from the most amazing, enlightening experience any human being can have happen!

How many people can say that they have seen Divine Consciousness incarnated in the flesh? Now the question is, "What do I do with it?" I think, in fact, I'm sure I shouldn't do anything, except let "it" do what it wants, when it wants. Like I said, I firmly believe that there is a time for planting seeds and there's a time for harvest. And right now, I can tell you that so many seeds have been planted inside of me that I feel pregnant on many levels.

It is my hope this story touches you in some way and helps you to believe and strive for that magic which abounds when you seek the highest truth and meaning. Believe me, my friend, the Divine is tangible and there for your taking.

You may ask, *"Should I seek out a holy man like you did and go to His ashram to have the experiences you've had?"* My answer is, no. It's all about the fire one has in their belly. Do you have the willingness to throw what you think is real or not into the Divine Flames to stoke a blaze within yourself?

I didn't log much about my trip home because there wasn't much to tell, except maybe two things:

One was something that came in a meditation followed by a manifestation.

Love is from what we emerge.
In Love, we should submerge.
Into Love, again, we merge.

After using this as a mantra for about ten minutes, I felt compelled to randomly open up a book I bought in the ashram and lo' and behold, there it sits verbatim:

Love is from what we emerge.
In Love, we should submerge.
Into Love, again, we merge.

The other is that, when I got to the airport in Michigan, I had to unpack all of my things for an inspection. I begged the Customs Officer not to make me do that because of all the stuff I had, which made him even more insistent. After he finished digging through my things and giving me the all clear, I repacked and continued home to Memphis.

I slept most of the way, again, gently going over in my mind and heart the grace shed on me for the last two weeks. All the people I met on my journey were equally beautiful and Divine as the Master I went to see. What a great gift to be among so many people living in love, peace, purpose and bliss; that in and of itself was most integral to the experience.

Well, now that I'm home and settling in, I'm stoked to see what transpires as I get back to my daily life.

A month later …

With my apartment now decorated in all the things I bought and my shrine complete, I feel as if I'm still in India. So much Divine energy fills my home that, as soon people walk in, they are hit with a huge wave of It and they literally gasp. They tell me they are moved to a place of peacefulness that they've never felt before. It's so amazing to witness!

Let me describe to you what my apartment looks like.

I painted all the walls mint green which looks really cool against my black furniture. There are Christmas lights all around the top of the ceiling that I leave on a slow fade setting. Decorative vinery was used to hide the lights' wires, making everything nice and neat. I hung that big poster of Sai Baba over my fireplace in a frame donned with pretty garland, and on each side a sconce holds a pot with beautiful flowers.

Everywhere in the apartment there's something to see. When you look around, you'll notice Baba pictures in chronological order of His life. There are Buddha, Jesus, Krishna and Ganesh statues that sit on the shelf by the kitchen. I even went so far as to find some real bamboo and placed it in every corner of my home. I took a closet I didn't use anymore and turned it into an atrium now home for two finches: Sai, the female, and Baba, the male. And the fact that I have spiritual music always playing seems to push everything over the top. Now, maybe you have some idea of the ambience in the shrine to my Teacher.

Do You Believe?

It's been just over two months since I've returned from India and so many things have happened. Miracles are still occurring. Where do I begin?

Last night I went to world-famous Beale Street to play music. After my gig was over, I went walking with my girlfriend, Kimmie, looking for something to do. She had the idea to go to a psychic shop nearby for a reading. When her session was over, she talked me into getting one. I sat down and the lady psychic requested my name and birth date. She then immediately asked me, "Where in the world did you just come from?"

"I just got back from India. Why do you ask?"

"The bright light you are emanating is blinding me, making my head hurt and there is just no way I can read you!"

As you probably have guessed, I left the shop feeling blessed and validated.

Kimmie had also mentioned to me that since I've been back, whenever we are around each other, her head would hurt from an enormous pressure.

Last week, a friend named Amy came over for a visit wanting to know all about my trip to India. Once we got into the thick of it, she shouted, "Oh, my God, Keith! There is a bright, blue light surrounding your entire body." The phenomena happened to take place when I told her about my visit to the Krishna Temple in Mumbai. Anyone who knows anything about Krishna will tell you that His skin is always depicted as blue.

After the wow-ness of the blue light wore off, I told Amy about the almost full apparition of Krishna I had in Kulwant Hall, mentioned in the chapter, "Sai Ram, That Lady Is Me!" Even though she totally trusted me, Amy didn't know how to handle such a thing and decided to leave.

A week later, we spoke on the phone about what had taken place when she was at my apartment. Still uneasy about it all, Amy asked if we didn't speak of it whenever we were together.

Since I've been home, I can tell you that how I feel about myself has shifted. Although I'm still a devotee of Baba, I'm not as "obsessed" about Him as I used to be. My journey, my experience, my vision, my feelings, my expansion and my time with Lord Baba has become such a big part of who I am, that I can now feel a deeper integration taking place. It feels like I'm going from knowing that I am God, to actually feeling that Presence as me.

The miracles that I've witnessed while in India are continuing to unfold. But now, I'm getting much better at keeping up with them and what they represent. Day after day, the Grace from All That Is Good shows Its Beautiful Face, keeping me in a space of appreciation, expansion and elation.

Four months later ...

Boy does time fly when you are having fun! I've gotten so wrapped up in my life that four months have passed since I've written anything. But the writing bug got back into me because of an experience I had 45 minutes ago.

I was watching *Gilligan's Island* on the television, and after it was over, I felt compelled to go to a store down the road. But, for what, I didn't know. With no clue about why I was going there, I decided that I would fill up my little white Mitsubishi Sport Mighty Max truck with fuel. As I'm doing so, I noticed a man (using the payphone) and a woman sitting on bikes, clad in biking gear. "I know this man. Yes ... I know this man! But, from where?" This was puzzling me so much that I raised the hood of my truck and pretended to fidget with it until he was done.

After he hung up the receiver I said to him, "Excuse me, sir. Where do I know you from?" Wheeling over to me to get a closer look he said, "Oh, wow! You are the guy that sat next to me on the plane flying to South India." The realization of that moment not only hit me (and I'm used to it), but smacked him so hard he almost lost balance and fell off of his bike.

With such delight, the gentleman and I chatted for a bit about what just happened and what we'd been up to since that plane ride. After we shook hands and they both pedaled away, I got in my truck and drove home as fast as I could to write down this amazing alignment.

What do you think about that? How does it feel to you to hear such a story? Can you imagine that all you have read in this book is true? That is the question. DO YOU BELIEVE? That's your choice. In fact, it's the only choice you really have! What else is there? The idea that it is possible is what will allow you to claim what belongs to you. Do you get it?

Whether you believe what I experience to this point is real or not has no bearing whatsoever on the magic that frequently occurs in my life.

Do you believe all the miracles that have happened to me can happen to you?

Clarity

Are you beginning to see your healing process in action, My Friend?
"Yes, very much so!"

My aim, no matter what may be placed before you, is to always
bring out the Divine in you. How you yourself choose to deal with your
trials and tribulations is another matter entirely. As you get closer to
the core of who you really are, the more clarity will you have to deal
with anything.

Clarity
Clearness (in various senses).
The condition of being clean
and free of contaminants.

Absolute clarity is one of My grandest attributes. For you to have
it too will require crystal clear intention – a lifelong commitment
of your spirit, mind and body – your feelings, thoughts and
actions – constantly working to dislodge and discard all beliefs
that block clarity's light. Every time you employ discipline and
dedication, you will be getting closer to Me at a conscious level.
I shall now show you an excellent way to begin this process.

When you awaken each morning, stay supine for a few
moments. Go over the dreams you had while your body was
at rest. As you start to interpret these mind movies, how you
feel about them will let you know whether or not you are clear.
Then you will know how to adjust your visualizations so you
can intentfully plan the way you wish your day to go. Your clear
intent and positive attitude will set the tone, and the day you
desire will unfold.

Each evening just before you go to sleep, think about what did
not align with your morning's visualizations, and be grateful for
all that did. Then ask for the clarity to fine-tune your prayers and

intentions so that tomorrow will be a better day. As soon as you can determine what to do and what not to do in any situation, living a peaceful life will become second nature.

Keith, you have always had creative power. What has kept you from maximizing it has been your cluttered mind. Why not look at your creative process like this:

You are a movie projector and God is the Light inside. Your thoughts are the film itself. As you sit in the theater of life, what movie is playing on that 3D screen of yours? A horror flick? If so, change the film!

The simple fact is that, conscious of it or not, you are the producer and director of your own movie, and any sad or unfinished scene in it will only become more difficult to wrap if you do not take responsibility for its content.

Is your life playing out the way you want it to? If not, the only way to get it to go the way you truly desire is to do the work necessary and get clear about it. That is the crux of it – no more, no less. Neither good nor bad. Your life is the movie you make.

Do you sometimes get frustrated because things do not seem to work out the way you intended?

"Yeah, for a long time my life has been filled with frustration and confusion. Up until the last few years, I didn't know it all spawned from my intentions."

I will tell you this: You have gotten and are getting exactly what you have intended. With whatever degree of clarity you have had, you have intended. Even if someone does not make a choice, still a choice is made – the choice to remain complacent. Thus do the patterns of sameness evolve – by unaware intentions.

For those who accept and apply the wisdom of this simple truth, life will get easier and more fulfilling. For those who do not, trouble will remain. Either way, everyone will go on creating. And either way, you will all get what you want.

"Well then, what I want is enlightenment!"

If you truly wish to bring perpetual Love into your daily life, becoming pure is imperative. Only then can Spirit lift you higher, so that the dive from your ego into Its Arms will be a graceful one. Once your clarification and elevation begin to accelerate, people will recognize that you are living with more joy. That will be your confirmation of the work you have been doing.

"Boy, I can't wait for that day to get here!"

Do not be in such a hurry, Keith! Where you are now is a normal part of the process. The goal is not the goal; the journey is. If you focus on the future, you will lose the power of the present moment.

"Why do I still find it hard to tell the difference between what's Spirit and what's my ego?"

Every aspirant on a spiritual path goes through this phase of not being able to tell for sure when the ego is dominating. But your not knowing says it loud and clear – the ego is still in charge. Yes, even though knowing is your natural state, you still sometimes depend on your ego for answers it is incapable of providing. You see, since the ego can never communicate with Spirit, it will always insist that it is you who is the incapable one. When it does that, doubt begins to creep in and you stray away from being the deliberate creator that you so want to be.

I am advising you to relax now, Dear One, for Spirit will provide you with what the ego cannot. Open, accept, be clear and know, and your life will speak for itself.

"But I still sometimes judge my lack of progress."

Ah, but the universe knows no lack! Believe it or not, what you may regard as lack is actually progress.

Everything always moves forward. Because you do not yet see evidence of this is evidence to Me that you are still in the progress process. Do not be so hard on yourself, Beloved. Give yourself some grace like I do.

Bit by bit – or by leaps and bounds – the clarity that comes to you will benefit not only you alone, but the people around you and the world as well, all of whom can use as much healing as you will be able to offer.

"Will You please share some of the universe's mechanics?"

Through this book, as well as many others, it has been established that Love is all there is and there is nothing else. Now I will explain how the mechanisms of Love sustain the whole universal system.

The universe rests upon the Divine Principles of Clarity and Love, which form the light grid through which Spirit travels. These two principles are what allow the Divine to be omnipresent. The good news is that you can hitch a ride with Spirit if you elect to abstain from your earthly bad habits and make that abstinence part of your routine.

"Do I dare ask … um … what do You suggest I work on?"

For starters, change your diet by eating less and by staying away from fast foods and cured meats. Include more fresh fruits and vegetables in your menus. Before long, you will be amazed at the added energy you have.

Besides being prone to eating poorly, you have taken on other bad habits along the way, dabbling in lots of things from the outside world that have provided you with quick thrills. But they have not satisfied you, because if they had, you would not have returned for a second (and third and fourth …) helping. Even now, any time you want some immediate gratification, your mind is more than willing to remind you of all the things that will give it to you. With cigarettes for example, you smoke one after another because the mind has you convinced that doing so will bring you some satisfaction.

Any and all addictions hamper growth because of the useless, monkey-mind noise they create – a noise so loud that Spirit's whisper gets lost in the din. Sad to say your vices will stick around until you find the clarity (mind silence) that will let you listen to Spirit.

"What about what addictions do to the body?"

Understand that the mind and body are not separate, for in

the empty space of body is mind. Actually, the body is the mind solidified. So if one part of the mind is ill (not clear), over time, what that part demands will begin to poison the body. And, over time, you will actually be able to observe your body manifest mind or Spirit, whichever one you have chosen to let govern your life.

The addictions I speak of here are the ones that affect people the most – cigarettes, drugs, alcohol, food, gambling and sex.

"But are we not allowed to experience those things?"

Yes, if you choose to. But problems set in when you have to have it, not when you are occasionally indulging in something simply to enhance your fun. But do not be fooled by the "I'm not an addict; I do it because I like doing it" tricks that the mind likes to play on you. You know where you stand, Keith. If you find that your addictions are getting the better of you, know that you have lost sight of your goal of Self-fulfillment.

"From now on, when my mind tells me that I need something, I'll try to pay more attention to what's really going on."

That would be good to do because every unhealthy habit or addiction you keep hold of only affirms that you intend to stay within the limits of earthbound reality. With each attempt to give up these vices, you take another step towards the clarity that will finally let your Higher Self settle into place.

Beloved, I tell you yet again that there is so much abundance within you. But how can you expect to see that when you are not yet clear?

"So You're telling me that the reason I've stayed so frustrated is because I haven't been able to realize Your Bounty and to manifest it? Is that it?"

Not only that. Your frustration has thrown your mind into ego overdrive and that, combined with your feelings of need, makes you think that you must "get it while the getting is good."

"Isn't this the way the world operates?"

Not entirely, but you are correct in one sense. There are many lack-minded corporations that refuse to let go of their need and greed to possess and monopolize. They are the primary reason the Earth's health has gotten so poor. If they are allowed to continue, their ongoing abuse of the planet will hasten her dying and death.

"What can we do to keep that from happening?"

The clearer everyone gets, the more effective you will become at removing their parasitic energy because you will be using your own God-given power to correct the seemingly irreversible damage they have done.

Everyone must shift from poverty thinking and feeling to prosperity thinking and feeling. When that happens, you will become a channel for abundance to return, radiate outward and help heal the beautiful planet. As you look upon Me as the Infinite Repository of Wisdom and Wealth, the world's revolution, resolution and evolution will begin, and lack will end.

"You mean there'll be no more starving people in the world?"

No, I mean you will no longer see these people as starving, but as nourished. It is this very shift in perception that will compel you to do what is next in sequential order – feed the world.

"So what You're saying is that there is no lack of anything anywhere?"

Lack is your point of view, My Friend, not Mine, and that point of view is the cause of all your quandaries. Why the world has not addressed the hunger problem more aggressively baffles Me!

"Have we insulted You?"

What "insults" Me is that you have done so little with all I have given you.

"But what about all the organizations that feed the hungry?"

Are there still starving people in the world?

"Yes."

Then you have done nothing but attempt to feed the hungry. Because the world still operates from lack, it thinks that enough is being done, but that belief only keeps you worshipping the almighty dollar instead of the Almighty within that can provide the world with everything it needs.

"From what You've said so far, it sounds to me as if we have to die before we can go through this spiritual transition. Is this true?"

No, that is not the case at all. But many are so caught up in their life's drama that all they know themselves to be must die in order for love, trust and clarity to be born – in order that they may live.

I am pleased to say that you are dying gracefully, Keith. And as long as you continue helping others and keep striving for clarity, you will one day be able to tap into the power that will let you manifest a body to live in whenever you want.

Look around, Keith. Can you see how everyone must come to clarity before the chaos can be dissipated?

"Clearly."

The more of you that take part in this process, the more you will be able to influence the time/space coordinate of your ascension. Yes, as many of you as possible must work through your chaos because, if you continue to feed your addictions, you will continue to deprive yourselves of Me, and your fear and confusion will be all that remain.

"Why is peace so difficult for us to get to?"

Many do not know what peace looks like because they make no effort at all to familiarize themselves with it. It cannot be said enough: It takes love, trust and clarity to live the peace that lies within you.

This is your moment, My Child. For lifetime after lifetime I have watched you work diligently so that you could be here now, preparing for this grandest time in history. Do not take this life for granted, lucky one, because there are many souls who still await the chance you have been given – human birth!

Clarity and Love are the building blocks that give the

universe its form and maintain its integrity. They are the code and law of which you must follow to become aware of Spirit's omnipotence, omniscience and omnipresence – a reality that is only accessible to those who are no longer within shouting or whispering distance of the ego's voice.

Infinite possibilities reside within you here and now, Beloved. Can you see them? Can you hear them? Can you feel them?

"I see, hear and feel much, but throughout it all, I still get confused."

You will be glad to know that whenever you get confused there is a way for you to become clear.

"Really? How?"

By doing just that. By asking Me! The clarity you seek will come when you repeatedly think of God and invoke My Name whenever you have concerns.

"Now I understand why I haven't been able to reach those higher realities as often as I'd like – it's because I'm still not completely clear. Did Christ, Buddha, Mohammed and other deities go through this same process of purification that I'm going through?"

Yes, they did. Everyone must go through this process before their Light can fully emerge.

Beloved, you have already observed your own clarity in action because every time your knowing process has broken through it has given you quick glimpses of your life's potential. You were usually not able to make much sense of these images, but the deepest part of you knew that all was in order.

"Yeah, that's happened to me several times – when I've been able to flash on what seemed to be my future. And You're right, I somehow knew that my life was surely going there."

Remember how tough it was to put that feeling into words?

"Yes, why's that?"

Because the experience was yours alone. Whenever you have such an experience (and this goes for life in general), what you must try to do is remove your beliefs from what you think is happening. Take care not to ground yourself in what you think is going on, because that will only lock it in. Toss the images around as much as you must – and I invite you to do so – but know that any restrictions such as your beliefs (fears) will only inhibit you and keep you in a state of non-elevation.

"One night years ago, when I was asleep, I had an incredible spiritual experience that filled me with utter bliss. Did it mean that, for a moment at least, I was without belief?"

Yes, Dear One, in that one glimpse, you did touch an aspect of your Soul. But though you have had those few moments that felt like nirvana, never claim that you have finally found Me, for this will only block you. Instead, continue to look for the deepest meaning in every reality. As you do, you will notice a powerful shift in your thoughts and feelings, a shift that will let you feel even more of that Higher Self ecstasy when you are awake.

"Yes, after that experience I felt so intuitive!"

Did you find that your mind was more frequently filled with thoughts that somehow did not seem to belong to you? And is this not what you are now experiencing with the writing of this information? Dear One, you are beginning to unify with the Mind of One where no one owns thought but Me. You have been growing your omniscient (psychic) gift all this time so that we can communicate telepathically now. Do you not agree that life is getting somewhat easier?

"Much!"

Making contact as you did and listening to guidance as you do has taken miles off your journey Homeward. But you must be careful not to become euphoric over the idea that everything you hear is guidance when you make these kinds of psychic shifts. You must be careful not to let the ego reinstate itself into your decision-making.

You may ask how to discern between the guidance and the thoughts that you wish were true, and how to keep yourself from falling into this mighty trap of uncertainty again and again.

"Help!"

There, there, My Child, it will be alright. Your goal should be to keep it simple, because your frustration when you do not will cancel any headway you have made. In times of uncertainty, show gratitude for the clarity you already have and call upon Spirit with all your heart to help you dissolve your doubt. I touched on this earlier in the chapter and now I will expand on what I have already said.

Ask yourself this important question: Is this true guidance or just something my ego is projecting? If you are asking such a question in the first place, you have already gotten your answer from Spirit – whatever it is, is not Spirit!

"Hang on. Are You saying that what I wish were true and true guidance can never be the same?"

I am not implying that guidance will not lead you to what you want. What I am saying is that as you work to develop your psychic gifts, the ego will be working just as hard to convince you that its voice is the voice of guidance and the only one you should be listening to. That darned ego will always try to throw a monkey wrench into the ol' Keith-machine, hoping to keep you from your happiness. So pay close attention to who is doing the talking!

"No wonder it sometimes feels like I'm losing my mind."

Oh, how I hope so, Dear One!

"What the ...?"

I shall explain.

Your mind is the root of all your blocks and problems. It contains way too much stuff that serve no purpose to you whatsoever. So you must lose your mind; purge it thoroughly until what you know as mind is lost.

Since you are just beginning your omni-development, I know this may be confusing for you. But if you are patient and persevere in your spiritual practice, all will blossom in its proper season. Just continue to be on the lookout for synchronicity in your life, for it will let you know for sure when your guides are the ones seeking your attention.

And, Keith, remember that growing your psychic abilities is not the goal. The goal is God, God, God! The abilities I grant are My gift to you so that, in time, they can become a powerful tool for your work. I want you to know I have faith that you will pull through this transition.

It is not the practices, props and other superstitions everyone has been accustomed to when worshipping that will lift you all towards conscious union; it is your sincerity. And believe it or not, as you develop your levels of spiritual mastery, you will no longer even need to pray.

"How could that possibly be?"

Up until now, you had to depend on prayer because your own Divine forces have been latent. However, when you have your own Love power, you will have the Will to accomplish for yourselves what you have always called upon Me to do.

Continue to use the rituals that you are familiar with if they help you to fall deeper into a meditative state; and if it helps you to stay humble, then by all means pray! Keith, I assure you that your need for these rituals will one day disappear. Meanwhile, just continue being sincere, for that is what will hasten your ego's demise.

"This may be off point, but can You tell me if there are benefits to being alive now rather than in earlier times?"

Yes, you have it much easier now. Those before you who sought enlightenment did not have one benefit you have: the readily accessible collective power of the awakening many. That power, properly channeled, can propel all of you right into the Divine.

The ones who reached enlightenment long ago had to overcome by themselves the pull of many dark forces – but they did it. Yes, Great Ones such as Moses, Buddha and Christ lit the

Divine Lamp of Love to illuminate the path for you.

Each time Teachers such as these achieved an advanced state of omniscience, omnipotence and omnipresence, a potent burst of energy was released upon the lower strata. If you study Scripture, you will see that it points to yet other Divine comings, indicating that Teachers of this magnitude have not finished visiting Earth.

One such coming, Sathya Sai Baba, has attracted millions to bear witness. They have come to South India from all around the world to see Me, hear Me, feel Me and know Me through this Avatar (Divine Descent) – to see evidence of My Love and Grace in this human incarnation.

When these pilgrims return home from India, the brilliant burst of Light they were saturated with affects others, whether or not they share stories of the miracles they beheld. Thus Sai Baba's beam is able to radiate far beyond His physical location. Even so, many people will question the existence of this Avatar, to say nothing of His work and some of the things that take place around Him. From the Western point of view, the very idea of this particular embodiment of Mine will be seen by many as nothing but wrong.

"My own experience sure helps me to understand how that could happen."

When you (or anyone who has seen Sai Baba for him/herself) tell people that this Avatar creates objects out of thin air and is able to resurrect people ... well, you tell Me, Keith, how do they respond?

"They usually react with fear and disbelief."

Yet, after hearing of My arrival from others, many have gone to the ashram in India to observe with their own eyes what Sai Baba is up to. Some go with unaware intentions and have learned valuable lessons. These lessons I provide without judgment and in all Love. Some of these curious ones return home to share Sai Baba tales that are good and some return to tell ones that are not so good.

But those who go and then question Sathya Sai Baba's authenticity do not understand the mission of this Avatar. Or, perhaps, they are simply not yet willing to believe that what is happening is really happening and is for their betterment – for God's sake.

Let Me say here that all suspicions about My incarnation as Baba are good, for questioning encourages the search for answers. And let Me further say that there is a reason for everything that takes place at the ashram. That reason is to help everyone there to complete past karma and to find Me within themselves so that they will no longer worship God as another! There is no other reason.

"I've been to the ashram and my experience was completely divine! I was able to touch my Soul while I was there and for that I will always be grateful."

You have such good things to say about your trip to Sai Baba, Beloved, because, for the most part, your karma is good. And it is for this same reason that I have selected you as one of My scribes. Those with less commendatory stories are just on a different path.

"Thank You so much for helping me understand that part of Sathya Sai Baba's mission is to help others see who they really are, even at the expense of His own reputation. What an unselfish act!"

You are welcome!

Later on, I shall speak of yet another Divine incarnation that will come to the continent of America.

"Wow! I'll be looking forward to that."

It is because of incarnations such as Sathya Sai Baba that the world can be lifted out of darkness and human elevation can be made possible. Yes, Dear Ones, since you are no different from these Masters, not only is it possible for each of you to reach their level in your lifetime, it is your duty.

But do not be fooled into thinking that all you need to do is process a little here and a little there, and – Boom! – you are God-conscious. Granted, your pure and genuine intent is important, but there is much to iron out before you can become fully illumined. For example, you must still work on the karmic patterns both from your past lives and your current life's past. You do that by doing what I recommend, by expanding the Love within you until you consciously reach the level that is God. To reduce the risk of moving backwards, you must "keep on truckin'," knowing that I walk beside you and you never again have to be afraid.

Keith, I see you wanting to get higher but as the many aspects of your life are becoming finalized, I also observe the fear that is causing you to resist the changes that are taking place. My Son, change is inevitable! Just wait and see – the more you close the old doors of your life, the more new ones will open for you.

"So, how do I get comfortable enough, despite my fears, to walk confidently through them?"

All you can do is prepare yourself for what may lie ahead. The clearer you become by doing Self-work, the fewer fears will crop up and, no matter what door you find yourself approaching, you will begin to recognize it for the opportunity it is. Indeed, as the path you are seeking begins to announce itself with more and more certainty, you will not feel comfortable unless you walk it. You already know this! This search you have embarked upon pulls at your heartstrings. It nudges you to keep moving towards God's Peace.

"But what if it turns out that I'm not on the right path?"

This is a common worry for most spiritual aspirants. But the truth is that no one can ever get off the path that is meant for him or her. If someone feels that they have strayed, this concern of theirs will put them right back on it.

Here is the path: Just stay in the present moment at all times. It is this awareness of the now that will keep you from being caught off guard by events that, in the past, would have caused you to react. It is not accurate to think that you can deviate from your life's design. The fact is that not recognizing the path is actually part of your path.

No matter what road you take, your life is in My Hands. But when you worry and try to control your life, it is as if you are trying to yank it out of My Hands – insinuating that I cannot do the job well enough. If that is your position, I assure you there will come a day when you will wish that you had trusted Me (Higher Self) from the very beginning.

"But it's such a challenge for me to let go of my wants."

You are not alone. There are many that think they know what will give them peace. But yet, even when they get what they think will do it, it turns out that peace is not a permanent part of the package. Tell Me, Keith, why do you think peace is so difficult for people to reach?

"Because somehow all of our wanting has managed to divert us away from You."

You have listened well. Have there not been times when you tried and tried to get what you wanted until you were utterly frustrated?

"Yeah. I would get tired of trying and say, 'Ah, forget it!'"

And how many times have you thought that what you wanted was never going to show up, only to hear Me say, "Here it is!"? You see, peace was there for you all along, but until you decided to release your self-inflicted burden of want, all you got for your efforts was a stressed mind, emotional conflict and physical exhaustion. For what reason? Beats Me!

I speak now to all My Children: What you must understand before you can fulfill your passions is the difference between wants and desires. I know this may sound contradictory, but it is not, because wants are "having to have" energies and desires are "God, You are my peace and if it is Your Will, this would be nice" energies. When you believe the former will bring you peace, rather than God who is Peace Itself, you negate any chance that your desires will be fulfilled.

When you choose God as the primary force and focus in your life, all things move toward you, not only because of the magnetic light you radiate, but because, within God, all things exist. As soon as you allow Me to take up full-time residence in both your mind and your heart, you will flourish.

Now on to true faith. When you achieve explosive clarity, you will have it. And along with it will come the power you need to manifest an ideal life. Faith, Clarity and Power: three facets of My Loom of Life, working together to weave all of Creation. These three cannot be separated lest all of them cease to be. Their immutable threads spin the Omnipresent Tapestry of Conscious Awareness that becomes a Divine Garment for all to don.

Do you see the glorious pattern I am constructing here?

"I think You're talking about unity."

Yes, the mighty power of all working together to benefit the All to bring about change. It should not be hard for anyone to see that two is mightier than one, three mightier than two, four mightier than three – to the Infinity that is God – One.

Faith not only describes belief in a particular religion, it also conveys one's hope for a particular outcome. Those who assume that results will come through blind faith cannot see how the power to manifest only springs from absolute knowing. Yet they are willing to gamble that their expectations will pay off – that they will hit life's jackpot – without realizing that they have nothing at all to back up their bet.

A believer hopes that his or her life will happen; a knower makes it happen by having the faith-supported gumption to go about living it. For some, their belief can be a crutch for laziness. But if you want it to, belief can easily become the catalyst to expand you into absolute knowing.

Faith can also be applied to the principle of believing in

something higher than you. This is but a metaphor because there is nothing higher than you. Many will say, "But this sounds like blasphemy!" I know that pondering such a thought may frighten many and may put religious leaders in a state of God-panic. So to them, I ask: How can such a beautiful thought about the Divine nature of all generate such fear?

"Well, haven't many religions taught that we are less than the Divine beings?"

Just because they say you are inferior does not mean that you are, for I have created no one above or below another. I do not separate nor favor anything, nor am I for or opposed to anything. If I operated this way, I would not be the Unity that I am. To clear up this misconception is the purpose of our transcription. That is: to help you to see all things through the eyes of Love.

"So what's it like to see and to be in this supreme state?"

Simply divine, My Keith! So crystal clear is My vision that everywhere I look, all I see is Me! I am not *the* supreme being. I Am Supreme Being, and My Beingness permeates everything in creation like light moving through glass.

"Is everything crystalline in structure?"

Yes, that is correct. From My Mind, all information passes through fiber-optic light branches to manifest everything everywhere all at once – illuminating Me as the Source of All that Is. By purifying that within you which remains clouded and constricted by fear, you, too, will come to see and be in this state.

"What a great session this was for me! I do believe I have much more clarity now."

I am very pleased to hear that, Keith, because if this chapter about clarity provided none, what would have been the point?

Just remember:

Call upon God in times of confusion.
Love is the power! Love is all there is.

Allow and accept yourself and all people.
Raise your vibrations by living My truths.
Intend to marry your God Self completely.
Trust that all things will unfold accordingly, according to –
You. It is all about you! Where there is clarity, there is
peace.

Come – See – Reflect

You want more information?
I've got tons of it; probably more than you'll ever need.

You want more knowledge?
I'll soon share more of what changed me.

You want more wisdom?
I'll soon share more of my life story.

You want more truth and a miracle?
Look in the mirror!

For now, we have come to the end of this reading journey. But before we part, do you see how over the course of my life, a solid connection with the Divine has been established? Good! What you are experiencing within yourself is your own initiation and integration of Spirit. Congratulations! As I, YOU, my Cosmic Sibling, have shifted.

Since the first page of this book, with words, passion, sincerity, humility and vulnerability, I have been imbuing you with the same Love and Light Fire that has set me ablaze, and forever it shall burn! There is no way anyone, not even you, can snuff that out. Run with it! You have the baton, the torch to illuminate your own path toward a transcended consciousness. My life story is a mere reflection revealing for you how with just a little bit of "elbow grease" and a lot of heart, you too can move into the final phase … GRADUATION!

You are loved beyond measure,
Keith Anthony Blanchard (YahNahVah)

About the Author

Reincarnated Avatar, Keith Anthony Blanchard was born on November 30, 1963, in Houma, Louisiana, and had a typical middle-class Catholic upbringing. In his early teens, he often entertained himself by pondering the big questions about God and the universe.

Little did he know that the day would come when those questions would form the spiritual foundation upon which he would build the rest of his life.

In his late twenties, Keith went through a crisis that stripped him of everything he held dear and left him with no choice but to turn inward for answers. This he did, but the peace and stability he so wanted still eluded him.

When he was 32, celestial beings began to appear to him, sharing glimpses of his future and the world's. Not only did they enlighten and guide him, they instructed him to pass their message on to others so that they, too, could learn a higher way of living.

Now in his fifties and living a peaceful, stable life, Keith continues to pursue his passion to both learn and teach about Truth.

Keith's credo:
Why choose to believe when you can know!

**6TH
BOOKS**

ALL THINGS PARANORMAL

Investigations, explanations and deliberations on the paranormal,
supernatural, explainable or unexplainable. 6th Books seeks to give
answers while nourishing the soul: whether making use
of the scientific model or anecdotal and fun, but always
beautifully written.
Titles cover everything within parapsychology: how to, lifestyles,
alternative medicine, beliefs, myths and theories.
If you have enjoyed this book, why not tell other readers by
posting a review on your preferred book site? Recent bestsellers
from 6th Books are:

The Afterlife Unveiled
What the Dead Are Telling us About Their World!
Stafford Betty
What happens after we die? Spirits speaking through mediums
know, and they want us to know. This book unveils their world…
Paperback: 978-1-84694-496-3 ebook: 978-1-84694-926-5

Spirit Release
Sue Allen
A guide to psychic attack, curses, witchcraft, spirit attachment,
possession, soul retrieval, haunting, deliverance, exorcism and
more, as taught at the College of Psychic Studies.
Paperback: 978-1-84694-033-0 ebook: 978-1-84694-651-6

I'm Still With You
True Stories of Healing Grief Through Spirit Communication
Carole J. Obley
A series of after-death spirit communications which uplift, comfort and heal, and show how love helps us grieve.
Paperback: 978-1-84694-107-8 ebook: 978-1-84694-639-4

Less Incomplete
A Guide to Experiencing the Human Condition Beyond the Physical Body
Sandie Gustus
Based on 40 years of scientific research, this book is a dynamic guide to understanding life beyond the physical body.
Paperback: 978-1-84694-351-5 ebook: 978-1-84694-892-3

Advanced Psychic Development
Becky Walsh
Learn how to practise as a professional, contemporary spiritual medium.
Paperback: 978-1-84694-062-0 ebook: 978-1-78099-941-8

Astral Projection Made Easy
and overcoming the fear of death
Stephanie June Sorrell
From the popular Made Easy series, *Astral Projection Made Easy* helps to eliminate the fear of death, through discussion of life beyond the physical body.
Paperback: 978-1-84694-611-0 ebook: 978-1-78099-225-9

The Miracle Workers Handbook
Seven Levels of Power and Manifestation of the Virgin Mary
Sherrie Dillard
Learn how to invoke the Virgin Mary's presence, communicate with her, receive her grace and miracles and become a miracle worker.
Paperback: 978-1-84694-920-3 ebook: 978-1-84694-921-0

Divine Guidance
The Answers You Need to Make Miracles
Stephanie J. King
Ask any question and the answer will be presented, like a direct line to higher realms... *Divine Guidance* helps you to regain control over your own journey through life.
Paperback: 978-1-78099-794-0 ebook: 978-1-78099-793-3

The End of Death
How Near-Death Experiences Prove the Afterlife
Admir Serrano
A compelling examination of the phenomena of Near-Death Experiences.
Paperback: 978-1-78279-233-8 ebook: 978-1-78279-232-1

The Psychic & Spiritual Awareness Manual
A Guide to DIY Enlightenment
Kevin West
Discover practical ways of empowering yourself by unlocking your psychic awareness, through the Spiritualist and New Age approach.
Paperback: 978-1-78279-397-7 ebook: 978-1-78279-396-0

An Angels' Guide to Working with the Power of Light
Laura Newbury
Discovering her ability to communicate with angels, Laura
Newbury records her inspirational messages of guidance and
answers to universal questions.
Paperback: 978-1-84694-908-1 ebook: 978-1-84694-909-8

The Audible Life Stream
Ancient Secret of Dying While Living
Alistair Conwell
The secret to unlocking your purpose in life is to solve the mystery
of death, while still living.
Paperback: 978-1-84694-329-4 ebook: 978-1-78535-297-3

Beyond Photography
Encounters with Orbs, Angels and Mysterious Light Forms!
John Pickering, Katie Hall
Orbs have been appearing all over the world in recent years. This
is the personal account of one couple's experience of this new
phenomenon.
Paperback: 978-1-90504-790-1

Blissfully Dead
Life Lessons from the Other Side
Melita Harvey
The spirit of Janelle, a former actress, takes the reader on a
fascinating and insightful journey from the mind to the heart.
Paperback: 978-1-78535-078-8 ebook: 978-1-78535-079-5

Does It Rain in Other Dimensions?
A True Story of Alien Encounters
Mike Oram
We have neighbors in the universe. This book describes one man's
experience of communicating with other-dimensional and extra-

terrestrial beings over a 50-year period.
Paperback: 978-1-84694-054-5

Dreamer
20 Years of Psychic Dreams and How They Changed My Life
Andrew Paquette
A ground-breaking, expectation-shattering psychic dream book
unlike any other.
Paperback: 978-1-84694-502-1 ebook: 978-1-84694-728-5

Electronic Voices: Contact with Another Dimension?
Anabela Mourato Cardoso
Career diplomat and experimenter Dr Anabela Cardoso covers
the latest research into Instrumental Transcommunication and
Electronic Voice Phenomena.
Paperback: 978-1-84694-363-8

The Hidden Secrets of a Modern Seer
Cher Chevalier
An account of near death experiences, psychic battles between
good and evil, multidimensional experiences and Demons and
Angelic Helpers.
Paperback: 978-1-84694-307-2 ebook: 978-1-78099-058-3

Spiritwalking
The Definitive Guide to Living and Working with the Unseen
Poppy Palin
Drawing together the wild craft of the shamanic practitioner and
the wise counsel of the medium or psychic, *Spiritwalking* takes
the reader through a practical course in becoming an effective,
empathic spiritwalker.
Paperback: 978-1-84694-031-6